A NOTE FROM THE MUSEUM OF THE ROCKIES

Dear Readers:

Why are children so intrigued by dinosaurs? Perhaps it is because dinosaurs seem so different from anything that exists today. Perhaps it is because some were so big. There is no land animal living on earth today that compares in size to Tyrannosaurus rex or Seismosaurus.

Lately, dinosaurs have been receiving unprecedented attention. News of spectacular finds by paleontologists around the world have rekindled our interest in them. The magic of film, books, and museum exhibits have also helped bring them back to life to scare and delight us as never before. But often, the information provided about these animals flies in the face of what paleontologists have worked so hard to find out about them. For children today, it is sometimes difficult to separate dinosaur theory from fantasy.

That's where this book comes in. It was created to offer you and your students a fresh look at dinosaurs, based on the very latest discoveries and hypotheses. Its goal is to provide accurate information about these incredible animals--and the scientific research behind them—through a series of fun, hands-on activities.

We hope you enjoy using this book...we certainly enjoyed writing it for you!

Sincerely,

Bonnie Sachatello-Sawyer

Bonnie Sachatello-Sawyer
Museum of the Rockies
Director of Education

Museum staff at a dig site

5

LAUNCHING A DINOSAUR THEME UNIT

Welcome to *Dinosaurs!* This resource was created to help make the study of dinosaurs a meaningful, fun, and organized learning experience for you and your students. There is no right or wrong way to use this book—or to launch a dinosaur theme unit—but here are a few tips to consider before getting started.

1 Invite students to help design your dinosaur theme unit.
A KWL chart will assist you in determining what kids *really* want to know about dinosaurs (see page 14). For example, you may find your students are far more interested in the anatomy of T. rex than the finer points of continental drift. That's okay. Be attentive to children's big questions about dinosaurs and use them to determine an appropriate—and motivating—focus for your theme unit.

2 Choose activities that will support your students' interests and the content areas you wish to teach. Should you try to do all the activities in this book? Probably not. Instead, we suggest that you graze through it with an eye toward selecting the projects that will mesh with your students' interests and learning styles, as well as the content areas you wish to teach. Although *Dinosaurs* is structured so that the activities can be done in the sequence presented, we encourage you to move from section to section to suit your own needs. Feel free to adapt, amend, or develop new projects to support you class's natural course of learning. After all, you know your students best!

3 Round out your study of dinosaurs with lots of trade books. To enrich your exploration of dinosaurs, try pulling together a classroom library of nonfiction and fiction titles, appropriate for all reading levels (see Dinosaur Resource List on page 111 for some suggestions). If you like, ask the school librarian, parents, or your students to help you. Then, throughout the course of your theme unit, be sure to set aside quiet time for kids to devour books about their favorite dinosaurs. And don't forget the read-alouds—children are never too old to listen to a good story.

4 Celebrate your dinosaur theme unit as you go. Honor what students are learning about these fascinating creatures by featuring kids' work on bulletin boards, hall displays, and discovery tables. Enlist volunteers to make a Jurassic mural or life-sized, papier-maché *Velociraptor.* Steep your classroom in dinosaurs!

5 Encourage students to demonstrate what they've learned about dinosaurs with a culminating activity. As your theme unit draws to a close, invite children to dig deeper into dinosaur science by choosing a research project to pursue on their own, with a partner, or in a cooperative group (see page 100 for some ideas). And don't forget to give students plenty of opportunities to share their knowledge with fellow students and parents—they love being the experts!

6 Invite kids to keep on learning about dinosaurs. Your students may never out-grow this wonderfully rich topic. Continue to spotlight appropriate newspaper and magazine articles with the class after you complete your theme unit.

Dinosaurs

THE VERY LATEST INFORMATION AND HANDS-ON ACTIVITIES FROM THE MUSEUM OF THE ROCKIES

by Liza Charlesworth
and Bonnie Sachatello-Sawyer

SCHOLASTIC
PROFESSIONAL BOOKS

New York • Toronto • London • Auckland • Sydney

DEDICATIONS

For my sister Jacqueline,
who I'll always look up to
—L.C.

For my parents,
who introduced me to museums
—B.S.S.

ACKNOWLEDGMENTS

This book would not have been possible without the expertise of many museum staff including Dr. Jack Horner, Patrick Leiggi, Sharon Horrigan, Frankie Jackson, Kristin Junette, Dr. Desmond Maxwell, Bruce Selyem, Dr. David Varricchio, and Arthur Wolf.

Cover design by Frank Maiocco

Interior design by Jo-Ann Rosiello

Illustration by Edward Heck and James Hale

Technical Illustration by Jo-Ann Rosiello

Photos by Museum of the Rockies, Inc.

ISBN 0-590-49412-0

CONTENTS

UNDERSTANDING PALEONTOLOGY

THE SCIENCE OF STUDYING DINOSAUR FOSSILS

WELCOME TO THE WORLD OF DINOSAURS

What is a dinosaur?

Dinosaurs were a special group of animals that roamed the Earth long ago. Their fossil remains suggest that they were very closely related to ancient and modern-day birds. In fact, a number of paleontologists now believe that birds actually evolved from dinosaurs. Dinosaurs can be described by the following five important characteristics.

1 **All dinosaur lived during the Mesozoic Era, 245 to 65 million years ago.** However, not all animals that lived during this time were dinosaurs. Dinosaurs lived in varied ecological communities along with an abundance of other creatures, including mammals, amphibians, and insects.

2 **All dinosaurs lived on land.** While some dinosaurs might have been able to wade or paddle through water, they did not live in oceans, lakes, or rivers. Mosasaurs and plesiosaurs, the giant swimming reptiles that also lived during the Mesozoic Era, were not dinosaurs. Nor were the ancient flying reptiles, known as pterosaurs.

3 **All dinosaurs were vertebrates.** Large or small, dinosaurs were all backboned animals that shared similar skeletal features.

4 **All dinosaurs walked with their legs positioned directly underneath their bodies, like birds.** This adaptation made dinosaurs efficient walkers and runners, and was very likely one of the keys to their long-term survival.

5 **All dinosaurs were diapsids, meaning they had two holes in their skull located behind their eyes.** These holes helped to lighten their skulls and provided important attachment places for facial muscles.

Devouring Misperceptions

▶ *Dinosaurs did not live with humans.*

▶ *Pterosaurs, the flying reptiles, were not dinosaurs.*

▶ *Dinosaurs did not live in the water.*

▶ *Dinosaurs were not cold-blooded.*

▶ *Dinosaurs did not have pea-sized brains.*

▶ *Dinosaurs did not drag their tails on the ground.*

▶ *Most species did not spend the majority of their time killing one another.*

What is paleontology?

Paleontology is the study of ancient life forms. The type of scientist that studies these fossil remains is called a *paleontologist*. Not all paleontologists study dinosaurs. Some study ancient invertebrates (animals without backbones), such as clams, turtles, and snails. Others study vertebrates, such as fish, swimming reptiles, and early mammals. Paleobotanists are scientists who study extinct plants.

At the Museum of the Rockies, the staff specializes in the study of dinosaurs and other animals that lived during the Mesozoic Era, including frogs, lizards, rodents, birds, and flying reptiles.

Meet Paleontologist Dr. Jack Horner

The Museum's curator of paleontology is Dr. Jack Horner. Jack, who was born in Shelby, Montana, has collected dinosaur bones all his life. In fact, at age 7, he displayed his first collection in the basement of his boyhood home. In 1978, Jack made history by identifying some of the first dinosaur nests and eggs in North America. The site, located near Choteau, Montana, also yielded babies and adult *Maiasaura*. Jack's find, and subsequent research determined that these animals nested in colonies and cared for their young. Prior to this, it was believed that dinosaurs abandoned their babies once they had hatched, as modern-day reptiles do. Today, Jack continues his research on this site and others throughout Montana. His mission is to find out what these animals' lives were like millions of years ago.

Paleontologist at a Montana dig site

When was the first dinosaur discovered?

Way back in 1676, Robert Plot, the curator of an English museum, described and drew a thigh bone that he believed belonged to a giant man. Although that fossil disappeared without a trace, the surviving illustration suggests that it may well have been part of a *Megalosaurus.* Later, in 1822, large teeth discovered in England by Mary Ann Mantell and her husband, Gideon, were thought to be the remains of a huge and extinct iguana. It wasn't until 1841 that British scientist Richard Owen came to realize that such fossils were distinct from the teeth or bones of any living creature. The ancient animals were so different, in fact, that they deserved their own name. So Owen dubbed the group *Dinosauria,* which means "terrible lizards."

Across the ocean in North America, dinosaur tracks were studied in the Connecticut Valley, beginning in the 1830's. They were believed to belong to enormous ravens, freed from Noah's Ark after the Great Flood. At that time, paleontology was long on deduction and short on evidence. This was remedied when two wealthy and competitive American scientists, Othniel Marsh and

That's a Fact!

In ancient China, dinosaur fossils were thought to be the bones of dragons. Back then, people crushed up these fossils and used them to make medicine and magic potions.

That's a Fact!

In the "olden days" dinosaur bones were mistakenly believed to belong to:

▶ *dragons*

▶ *giant people*

▶ *huge birds*

▶ *enormous, extinct lizards*

▶ *monsters*

Edward Cope, raced to excavate fossils in the Rocky Mountain region. In the late 1800's, their separate teams, armed against Native Americans and each other, dug up tons of bones from several sites. All in all, Marsh and Cope's rivalry—known as the Bone Wars—uncovered 136 new species. And their respective fossil displays generated excitement for dinosaurs the world over.

In the 1900's, enthusiasm for dinosaurs grew steadily, attracting the attention of the scientific community. Institutions such as the Carnegie Museum of Natural History and the American Museum of Natural History assembled dig teams, which uncovered many rich bone beds in North America (as did their counterparts overseas). New sites in Utah

Paleontologist prepares a fossil to go to the museum

FANTASTIC FINDS TIME LINE

1822
Mary Ann Mantell finds *Iguanodon* teeth in England. Her husband, Dr. Gideon Mantell publishes his description of them.

1841
Richard Owen coins the term *dinosaur.*

1855
Ferdinand Hayden discovers the first dinosaur remains in the United States.

1858
The first dinosaur skeleton, *Hadrosaurus,* is excavated in the United States and described by Joseph Leidy.

1890
Othniel Marsh and Edward Cope unearth 136 new species of dinosaurs in the Rocky Mountain region of the United States.

1902
Barnum Brown uncovers the first *Tyrannosaurus rex* specimen in Montana.

10

revealed several different species, including *Camarasaurus, Apatosaurus,* and *Stegosaurus*; *Tyrannosaurus rex* remains were found in Montana and baby Coelosaurs in New Mexico.

In recent decades, dinosaur research continues, but the emphasis has shifted from finding and classifying these animals to analyzing and reconstructing their lives and habitats. In the late 1960's, Robert Bakker proposed that these ancient creatures may well have been as agile and energetic as warm-blooded animals. In the mid 1970's, Peter Dodson, along with James Farlow, hypothesized that they used their horns to attract the attention of females, as well as for fighting. And in the late 1970's, Jack Horner made history by identifying some of the first dinosaur nests and eggs in North America. These important *Maiasaura* fossils helped to determine that some species nested in colonies and cared for their young.

In the past few years, several paleontologists, including Ken Carpenter, Phil Currie, and William Coombs, have identified juvenile dinosaurs that were previously thought to be adults; and David Weishampel has theorized that some dinosaurs probably used their crests and nasal passages to create sound. Each day, scientists working all over the world, in the field and in research labs, help to redefine the meaning of the word *dinosaur*.

1909

Earl Douglass discovers the fossil-rich rocks that are now Dinosaur National Monument.

1922

Roy Chapman Andrews finds the first dinosaur eggs and nest ever uncovered, in the Gobi Desert.

1960's

John Ostrom describes *Deinonychus* as an active and agile animal and suggests that birds are related to dinosaurs.

Dinosaurs are proven to have rigid tails that did not drag on the ground.

1970's

Research of thin sections of dinosaur bones suggests warm-bloodedness.

Bob Bakker and Peter Galton suggest birds and dinosaurs should be classified together as "Dinosauria."

1980's

Jack Horner and Bob Makela determine that some dinosaurs cared for their young.

Seismosaurus is uncovered in New Mexico by David Gillette.

1990's

Paul Serreno discovers some of the earliest-known dinosaurs.

Dinosaur fossils are found in Antarctica.

11

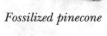

Fossilized pinecone

What was the dinosaurs' world like?

Dinosaurs, as a group of animals, lived on Earth from 245 to 65 million years ago, during the Mesozoic Era. They survived for an amazing 180 million years. Why did these animals thrive? Paleontologists aren't sure, but it is clear that over time dinosaurs evolved and adapted to a variety of ecosystems—living alongside insects, lizards, frogs, crocodiles, flying reptiles, birds, and mammals.

The **Mesozoic Era** (245 to 65 million years ago) is so long that it's divided into three parts: the Triassic, Jurassic, and Cretaceous Periods. During this era, the world went through a series of slow but radical changes.

At the beginning of the **Triassic Period** (245 to 208 million years ago), all of the continents were massed together, forming one supercontinent called *Pangaea*. It was during the Triassic Period that dinosaurs first appeared, evolving from their crocodile-like relatives. The oldest-known dinosaurs were fairly small, but their ability to walk with their legs underneath their bodies gave them the advantage of speed over their relatives. By the end of the late Triassic Period, Pangaea began to break up and there were many groups roaming the Earth, including *Plateosaurus*, *Procompsognathus*, and *Herrerasaurus*.

During the **Jurassic Period** (208 to 135 million years ago) the continents continued to break up (Africa began to separate from North America; India began splitting away from Africa and Antarctica). As the continents parted, dinosaurs were forced to adapt to new climates and environments. In the Jurassic Period, huge sauropods, such as *Brachiosaurus* and *Apatosaurus* appeared and thrived, as did armored dinosaurs like *Stegosaurus*. Birds and mammals also evolved.

By the beginning of the **Cretaceous Period** (135 to 65 million years ago) most of the continents had separated. Lands once joined were now far apart and many were covered by shallow seas. There was even a sea across the middle of North America! During the Cretaceous Period, dinosaurs diversified rapidly—especially the herbivores—as the first flowering plants appeared on Earth. While some species adapted to live in the chilly regions of Alaska, others grew accustomed to the desert environments of Central Asia. *Tyrannosaurus rex* and *Triceratops* appeared toward the end of this period and were among the very last dinosaurs alive.

The Dinosaurs' Changing World

TRIASSIC

During the Triassic Period, all the continents were joined. The Earth had heavy vegetation near coasts, lakes, and rivers, but desert in its interior.

JURASSIC

During the Jurassic Period, the continents gradually broke apart. The world was warm, moist, and full of green plants.

CRETACEOUS

During the Cretaceous Period, most of the continents had separated. The seasons became more pronounced, and flowering plants were more abundant.

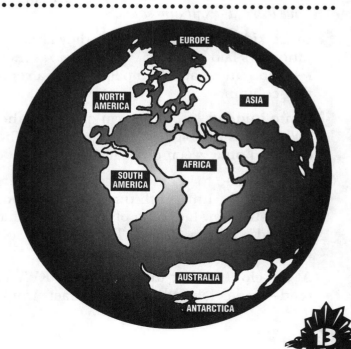

13

ACTIVITIES

Dinosaur KWL Chart (Language Arts)

This learning tool is the perfect springboard to the study of dinosaurs because it gives kids the opportunity to tap prior knowledge and choose the subtopics they want to know more about. A KWL chart (**K**: kids tell what they **know**; **W**: kids tell what they **want** to know; **L**: kids tell what they've **learned**) will help to ensure that your dinosaur unit is learner-centered—and exciting!

MATERIALS

▶ reproducible page 18
▶ red, green, and blue paper
▶ masking tape

DIRECTIONS

1 Use masking tape to divide a large wall space or bulletin board into three columns (making the third column about twice as big as each of the others). Label the first: *What we know about dinosaurs;* label the second: *What we want to know about dinosaurs;* label the third: *What we have learned about dinosaurs.*

What We Know About Dinosaurs	What We Want to Know About Dinosaurs	What We Have Learned About Dinosaurs

2 Invite kids to brainstorm facts they already know about dinosaurs, such as "Some dinosaurs laid eggs" or "*Tyrannosaurus rex* was a meat-eater." Record each fact on a red dinosaur shape (see page 18 for a reproducible pattern). Tape them in the first column.

3 Invite students to brainstorm questions they would like to have answered, such as: "Which was the biggest dinosaur?" or "Where did the dinosaurs live?" Record each question on a green dinosaur shape and tape them in the second column.

4 Now it's time to get cracking at the answers to those intriguing questions. Over the course of the unit, each time the class finds out an answer, write—or have students write—the new fact on a blue dinosaur shape and hang it in the "What we have learned" column. *Teacher Tip:* The facts you add to the third column need not be limited to the questions asked.

At the close of your unit, revisit the KWL chart by asking students to help you read—and celebrate—each dinofact. You'll be amazed at all the class has learned!

Picturing Dinosaurs: Poetry (Language Arts, Math)

Were all dinosaurs enormous? Answer that question and whet kids' appetite to study these incredible creatures with this fun, rhyming poem. Share "Picturing Dinosaurs" with the class by reading it aloud or copying it onto chart paper to recite chorally.

Picturing Dinosaurs

That Jurassic classic, *Ultrasaurus*—
imagine one is here before us:
    Line up three yellow school buses—
    You will know his length.
    Climb a building six stories tall—
    You will know his height.
    Put twenty elephants on scales—
    You will know his weight.

No one seems to make a fuss
about "elegant jaw" *Compsognathus.*
As the smallest, meat-eating dinosaur
he's one that you should not ignore:
    Just lay a yardstick on the floor—
    You will know his length.
    Think about a soft brown rabbit—
    You will know his height.
    Snuggle a kitten in your arms—
    Feel his weight!

by Bobbi Katz

© 1995 by Bobbi Katz

15

After enjoying the poem a few times, guide children to understand that not all dinosaurs were huge—in fact some, like *Compsognathus*, were pretty small. Next, ask students to brainstorm a list of land animals (elephant, mouse, squirrel, tiger, person, kitten, dog, ant, etc.). Write the names on a piece of chart paper, then challenge students to help you put them in sequence from biggest to smallest. (You may want to have some nonfiction animals books on hand to use as reference.) Where would *Ultrasaurus* and *Comsognathus* go? Are any of these animals bigger than *Ultrasaurus?* (no)

A rhino is smaller than an elephant

A zebra is smaller than a rhino

To Extend Learning

Invite kids to draw pictures of each animal on your list (in approximate scale) on separate sheets of paper. Then write captions under each, and bind them together to create a *Smaller and Smaller* book like the one on the left Put the book in your classroom library for kids to read and enjoy throughout the year.

Dinosaurs and You (Science)

Here's a great way for students to relate dinosaurs to their own world. Make double-sided photocopies of pages 19 and 20 (careful not to invert the image on the back of the page). Distribute one to each student. Have children begin with "Dinosaurs and You," which invites them to list some ways they are similar to and different from dinosaurs. When they're finished, they can hold their papers up to the light to see one of the most important things they have in common with dinosaurs—bones! Then have kids flip their papers over to "Dinosaurs and You, Part Two," where they are given the opportunity to learn the names of some important bones they share with the mighty dinosaurs. To prepare for this activity, you might encourage students to find these bones on their bodies, and practice saying their scientific names: *mandible* (jaw bone), *digit* (finger bone), and so on.

What Makes a Dinosaur a Dinosaur? (Science)

What makes a dinosaur special? How is it different from a lizard, a pterosaur, or any other living thing? To help kids understand what a dinosaur is (and *isn't!*), photocopy and distribute page 21 to each student. Read and discuss the four defining characteristics of a dinosaur. Then invite kids to use these facts to determine which of the pictured creatures *are* dinosaurs and color them green. Can kids think of any other qualities that make dinosaurs unique? Encourage them to share their ideas.

To Extend Learning

Invite kids to try moving around the room like dinosaurs and lizards. To imitate a dinosaur's gait, students should bend at the waist and walk normally, with their legs underneath their hips. To imitate a lizard, encourage students to pretend they are doing a pushup, then take a few steps forward. If you like, set the scene by playing special music, such as the "Theme from Jurassic Park." Ask: Which animal would you rather move like? Why?

Lizard   **Dinosaur**

Mesozoic Era Time Line (Science)

Explain to students that dinosaurs lived for an incredible 180 million years during the Mesozoic Era. The Mesozoic Era is divided into three periods: Triassic, Jurassic, and Cretaceous. Share information about these periods with kids, pointing out that different species lived during different periods. (For more information on the dinosaurs featured in this activity, see the Dinosaur Identification Cards on pages 57–62). Then illustrate this fact by inviting children to construct their own Mesozoic Era Time Lines. Here's how: Provide students with photocopies of pages 22 and 23. Ask children to cut out their time lines along the solid lines and assemble them as shown, then cut out the dinosaurs. Next challenge students to read each clue (for example, "I'm eating a plant"), match it with the correct dinosaur (*Plateosaurus*), and paste it in place.

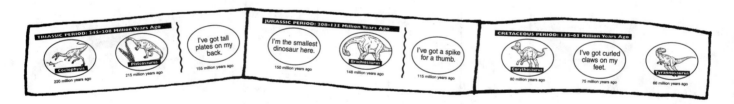

After kids have assembled their time lines, ask them to read the time lines by answering questions such as: Which is the earliest dinosaur shown? The latest? Which dinosaurs were alive during the Triassic period? Jurassic? Cretaceous? Which dinosaur lived 150 million years ago?

To Extend Learning

▶ Use the time line to reinforce math skills by posing questions such as: How many years long was the Triassic Period? Jurassic? Cretaceous? How many years earlier did *Coelophysis* live than *Brachiosaurus*?

▶ Add a strip of paper to the left-hand side of the time line to represent the Paleozoic Era (550 to 245 million years ago) and one to the right-hand side to represent the Cenozoic Era (65 million years ago to today). Challenge students to help you decide how long each strip should be. Then research the different creatures that lived during the Paleozoic Era (worms, jellyfish, and primitive reptiles, to name just a few) and what lived—and continues to live—during the Cenozoic Era (saber-toothed tigers and woolly mammoths—now extinct; cats, dogs, and us!).

Dinosaur Shapes

Reproduce this dinosaur to use with your KWL chart.

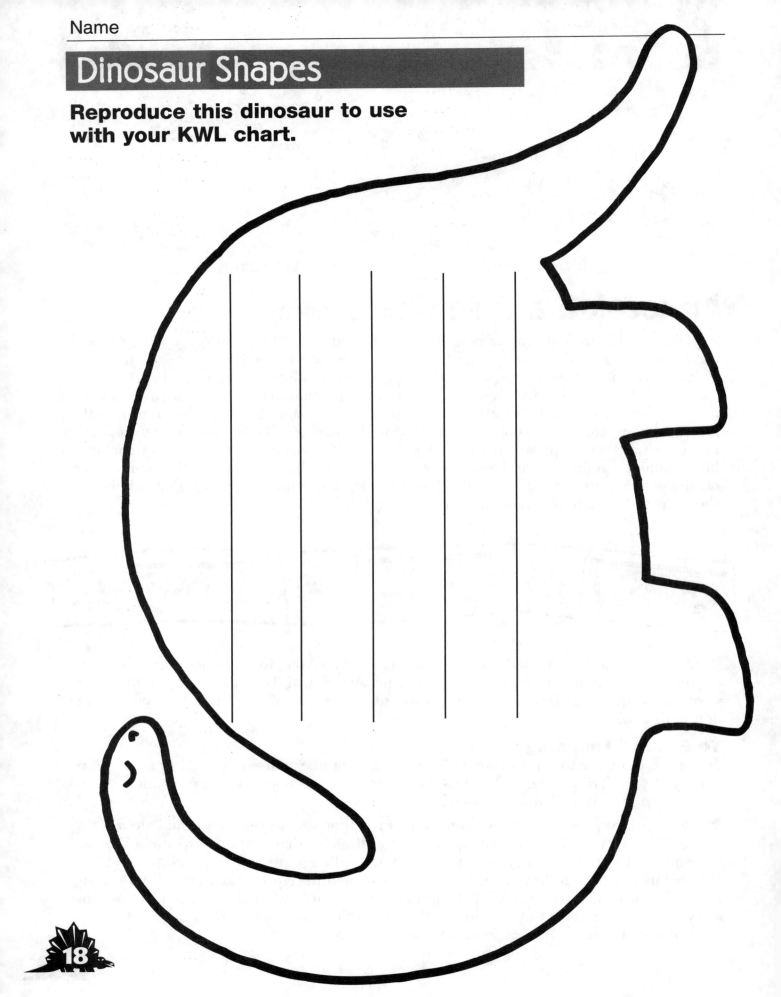

Dinosaurs and You

Maiasaura   **Person**

Dinosaurs roamed the Earth millions of years ago. You are alive today. But you and dinosaurs still have a lot in common. On the chart below, list some ways you are alike and some ways you are different.

ALIKE	DIFFERENT
We both have eyes.	People have hair.

 When you're done, hold this paper up to the light to see another way that you and dinosaurs are alike.

Dinosaurs and You (Part Two)

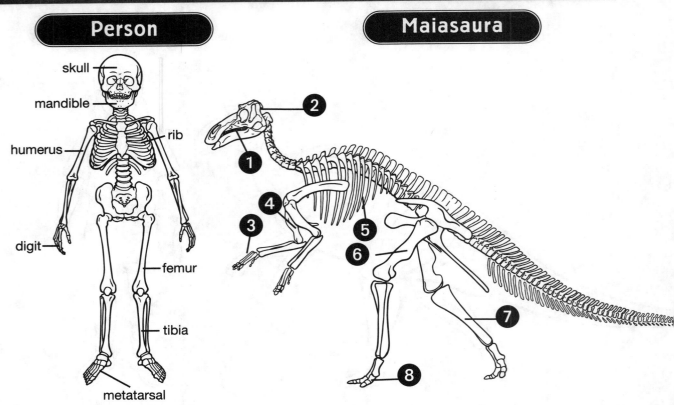

Person

skull
mandible
humerus
rib
digit
femur
tibia
metatarsal

Maiasaura

Look at the skeleton of the person. That's what you look like inside! Use it to label the same bones on the dinosaur.

Bone **1** is a ___mandible___

Bone **2** is a _____

Bone **3** is a _____

Bone **4** is a _____

Bone **5** is a _____

Bone **6** is a _____

Bone **7** is a _____

Bone **8** is a _____

Name _____

What Makes a Dinosaur a Dinosaur?

Use these four facts to tell which of the animals below are dinosaurs. Color only the dinosaurs green.

❶ Dinosaurs lived between 245 to 65 million years ago.

❷ Dinosaurs are now extinct.

❸ Dinosaurs lived on land.

❹ Dinosaurs could not fly.

Dimetrodon
lived 280 million years ago and are extinct

Woolly Mammoth
lived 5 million years ago and are extinct

Tyrannosaurus rex
lived 65 million years ago and are extinct

Triceratops
lived 70 million years ago and are extinct

Pteranodon
lived 75 million years ago and are extinct

Rhinoceros
are alive today

Crocodile
lived 210 million years ago and are alive today

Icthiosaur
lived 120 million years ago and are extinct

Spider
lived 200 million years ago and are alive today

DINO-CHALLENGE:

❶ Did dinosaurs live at the same time as people? _____

❷ Did dinosaurs live at the same time as spiders? _____

❸ Did dinosaurs survive longer than crocodiles? _____

Mesozoic Era Time Line

Cut out the time line along the solid lines so that you have three pieces. Paste the piece labeled "Jurassic Period" to the right-hand side of the "Triassic Period" piece. Then paste the "Cretaceous Period" piece to the right-hand side of the Jurassic Period" piece. When you're done, it should look like this:

TRIASSIC PERIOD: 245–208 Million Years Ago			JURASSIC PERIOD: 208–135 Million Years Ago			CRETACEOUS PERIOD: 135–65 Million Years Ago		
I'm chasing a lizard.	I'm eating a plant.	I've got tall plates on my back.	I'm the smallest dinosaur here.	I'm the biggest dinosaur here.	I've got a spike for a thumb.	I've got a big bump on my head, called a "crest."	I've got curled claws on my feet.	My nickname is T rex.
220 million years ago	215 million years ago	155 million years ago	150 million years ago	148 million years ago	115 million years ago	80 million years ago	75 million years ago	65 million years ago

Next cut out the dinosaurs on this page. Use the clues to match the dinosaurs to the times they lived, and paste them in place.

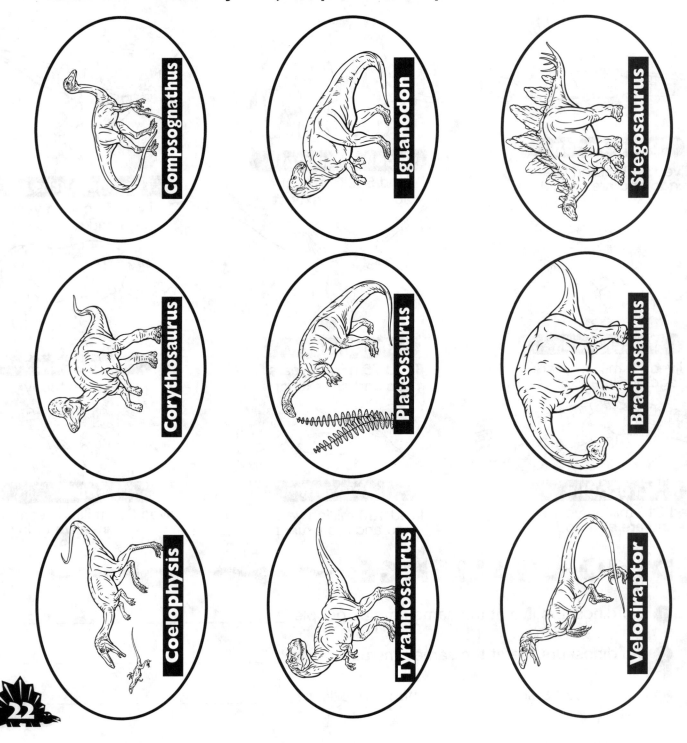

TRIASSIC PERIOD: 245–208 Million Years Ago

I'm chasing a lizard.

220 million years ago

I'm eating a plant.

215 million years ago

I've got tall plates on my back.

155 million years ago

JURASSIC PERIOD: 208–135 Million Years Ago

I'm the smallest dinosaur here.

150 million years ago

I'm the biggest dinosaur here.

148 million years ago

I've got a spike for a thumb.

115 million years ago

CRETACEOUS PERIOD: 135–65 Million Years Ago

I've got a big bump on my head, called a "crest."

80 million years ago

I've got curled claws on my feet.

75 million years ago

My nickname is T. rex.

66 million years ago

HOW THE DINOSAURS LIVED... AND DIED

Jack Horner on Dinosaurs' Color:

Some male dinosaurs may have had brightly colored crests to help them attract mates, but females probably did not. This color differentiation is also found in many modern-day birds.

What color were the dinosaurs?

While skin impressions have been found—suggesting a pebbly or scaly texture—no real dinosaur skin remains. That means paleontologists don't know for certain what color any of the dinosaurs were. They do have several theories, though. For example, many believe that dinosaur skin was probably drab shades of gray or green, allowing them to blend into their surrounding environments. This dull coloration would help them escape the detection of predators, enabling some to survive longer. Because large modern-day warm-blooded animals, such as elephants and rhinoceroses, tend to be dully colored, many scientists think that dinosaurs were, too.

But other paleontologists say the opposite is true—that dinosaurs' skin could have been shades of purple, orange, red, or even yellow with pink and blue spots! Rich and varied colors, they argue, might have helped dinosaurs to recognize one another and attract mates. Because research has shown that dinosaurs' closest living relatives—birds—can see in color, it is theorized that dinosaurs could, too. Scientists in this camp believe that color may well have been as important to these ancient creatures as it is to us.

Fossilized dinosaur skin shows texture, but no color

What did dinosaurs eat?

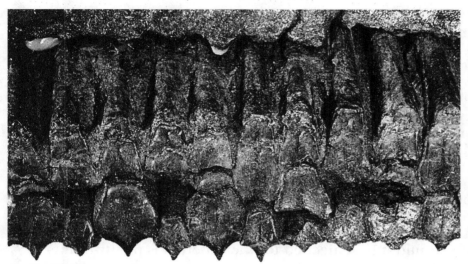

Fossilized Hadrosaur *teeth*

Although some fans of carnivorous *Tyrannosaurus rex* and *Velociraptor* may find it a bit disappointing—the vast majority of dinosaurs were plant-eaters. Most plant-eating dinosaurs had peg-like or broad, flat teeth designed for snipping or stripping vegetation. While the diet of individual herbivores varied, it likely included a combination of leaves, twigs, and seeds—found in high treetops or close to the ground. Some plant-eaters, like *Apatosaurus*, probably swallowed stones, which settled in their gizzards, helping to grind up the fibrous plant matter they consumed. These stomach stones, or *gastroliths,* are sometimes found among dinosaur bones at dig sites.

Then there were the carnivores. These dinosaurs' teeth—long, sharp, and serrated—were designed for tearing through tough meat. The eating habits of individual species no doubt varied, but probably included fellow dinosaurs, lizards, insects, and early mammals. Were the carnivores as fierce as they have been portrayed in the past? Yes and no. Paleontologists theorize that fast-running meat-eaters, such as *Velociraptor*, attacked and killed dinosaurs, then ate them. While others, like the infamous *Tyrannosaurus rex,* were likely scavengers, feeding on animals that had been killed by other dinosaurs or had died from natural causes.

Did any of the dinosaurs eat both plants and meat? Probably. Fossils show that certain species had different kinds of teeth—some for grinding and others for tearing—which suggests that they may well have feasted on both types of food. That would make these dinosaurs *omnivorous,* like us!

Fossilized Deinonychus *tooth*

A Feast Fit for a Beast!

These Mesozoic Era plants were probably food for many of the plant-eaters.

Horsetail

Fern

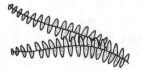

Pine

Pinecone

Magnolia

Gingko

The Great T. Rex Debate

Historically, T. rex has been considered "the king," but was this dinosaur a fierce predator...or a successful scavenger? The notion that T. rex was an active hunter is based on fossils suggesting that it had strong legs, long sharp teeth, a set of powerful jaws, and keen eyesight. But fossil evidence *also* suggests that T. rex's tiny, two-clawed arms were not even long enough to scratch its own chin. How then, some argue, could it have gripped and taken down another dinosaur?

Jack Horner thinks T. rex was a scavenger who used its massive size to scare other animals away from a site where prey already lay dead. Horner believes that in T. rex's day, there were probably many dead dinosaurs left behind after a herd departed. Even if T. rex had been a good hunter, why would it have needed to when there was plenty of meat for the taking?

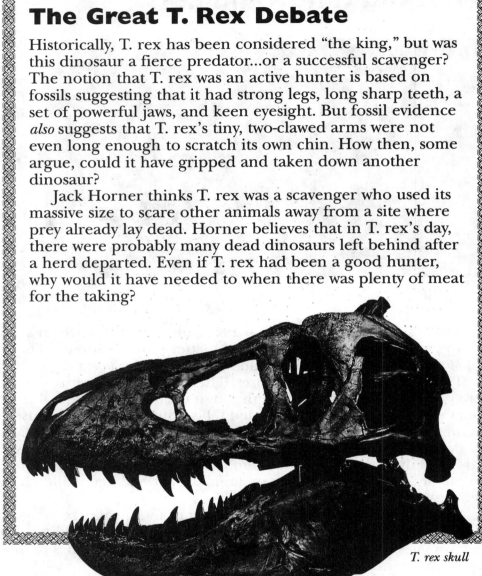

T. rex skull

Did dinosaurs walk on two or four legs?

By studying the skeletons and tracks of dinosaurs, paleontologists are learning more and more about how they moved. Fossil evidence suggests that many dinosaurs, such as *Brachiosaurus* and *Corythosaurus*, walked on four legs. While others, such as *Tyrannosaurus rex* and *Coelophysis*, walked on two. Still others were probably "convertible," or able to move on either two or four legs, depending on what they were doing. Dinosaurs such as *Plateosaurus* and *Iguanodon* most likely fell into this special category.

How fast did dinosaurs move?

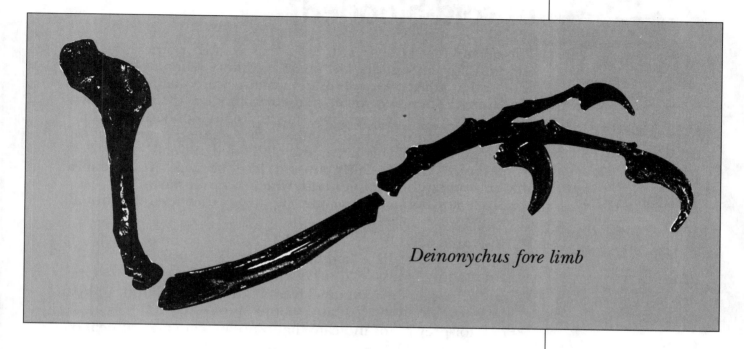

Deinonychus fore limb

While some dinosaurs were built for strength, others were built for speed. Evidence that certain dinosaurs probably ran fast is found by studying their fossilized leg bones and comparing these to the bones of animals that are alive today. Quick-moving, modern-day animals—such as deer and ostriches—tend to have long, slender leg bones with foot bones that are fused together for extra support. They run on their toes. Often the lower leg bones (the tibia and fibia) are longer than the thigh bone (the femur). Paleontologists study dinosaur fossils with these facts in mind. Those whose leg bones have a similar structure include *Troodon, Dromiceiomimus,* and *Chirostenotes,* which means that they were most likely pretty speedy.

How fast were they? All of these species could have easily outrun a person, so it's probably a good thing that we weren't around in the days of the dinosaurs!

That's a Fact!

One of the best ways to estimate the speed of dinosaurs is to study their fossilized tracks. Paleontologists think that Struthiomimus could have run 40 mph!

Jack Horner on Dinosaurs' Body Temperatures

We are now able to prove that some dinosaurs were warm-blooded, which distinguishes them from reptiles…and makes them a lot more interesting!

Were dinosaurs warm-blooded or cold-blooded?

The debate rages on! True there are as many hypotheses as there are dinosaur enthusiasts, but more and more paleontologists believe that at least some of the dinosaurs were warm-blooded or something in between warm- and cold-blooded. (Scientists now recognize varying degrees of warm- and cold-bloodedness.) In cold-blooded animals, body temperatures change depending on the temperature of the air. In warm-blooded animals, body temperatures stay at a fairly constant level because the animal is able to convert food into energy, which keeps it warm.

Some key points supporting the theory that several, if not all, dinosaurs were warm-blooded follow.

▶Dinosaurs could live in a range of climates, some of which would appear to have had too little sun and heat for cold-blooded animals to survive.

▶Some dinosaurs moved quickly and walked with an upright gait like warm-blooded birds and mammals of today.

▶Predator-prey ratios indicate that dinosaurs ate a great deal of food, as do modern-day, warm-blooded animals.

▶The bone structure of dinosaurs suggests that they were very active, like warm-blooded animals.

▶A recent study measuring the temperature of oxygen isotopes in several different bones of a dinosaur found them all to be at the same temperature, which supports the theory of warm-bloodedness.

Warm-blooded vs. Cold-blooded Animals

WARM-BLOODED ANIMALS

These animals have body temperatures that stay pretty much the same all the time. They produce their own body heat, or energy, from digested food. Because they are very active, they need to eat a lot.

COLD-BLOODED ANIMALS

These animals have body temperatures that change when the temperature outside changes: The sun warms them up and the shade cools them down. Because they are not very active, many can get by with a meal once a week or less.

What sounds did dinosaurs make?

Paleontologists may never know for sure what kinds of sounds dinosaurs made, but most believe that these animals did make noises. Why? Clues in dinosaur skulls tell them so. Some, like *Lambeosaurus*, had crests on top of their heads that probably filled with air when the animal breathed. As air was pushed through these crests, they likely made a deep bellowing sound similar to a horn.

Did dinosaurs communicate? Most paleontologists think so. Like modern-day birds and reptiles, dinosaurs probably made noises to signal that they were looking for a mate, that there was danger, or that they were hurt. Babies may have made sounds to let adults know they needed food or were in trouble.

While paleontologists have not found any evidence to suggest dinosaurs have external ears, the skulls and brain casts of certain dinosaurs indicate they had a good sense of hearing and the ability to hear both high- and low-frequency sounds. All of which mean their world could have been very noisy indeed!

Possible Dinosaur Sounds

➤ *bellows*
➤ *honks*
➤ *moos*
➤ *squeaks*
➤ *roars*
➤ *snarls*
➤ *snorts*
➤ *grunts*
➤ *hisses*
➤ *rumbles*
➤ *hoots*

Stegosaurus *spike*

Why did some dinosaurs have crests? Why did others have horns?

Crests and horns were probably used to help dinosaurs recognize others that were like them and to attract mates. And, when necessary, a dinosaur's horn might have come in handy to ward off predators. Were there other uses? Yes. Like most modern-day horned animals, such as a bison or bighorn sheep, male dinosaurs likely used their horns to jostle with one another in an effort to determine who was dominant. It is also believed that hollow crests helped dinosaurs make distinctive sounds.

The Best Crests

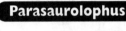
Parasaurolophus

Corythosaurus

Were dinosaurs social animals?

Paleontologists have uncovered large bone beds containing the remains of many of the same species of plant-eating dinosaurs. This indicates that some—if not many—dinosaurs were social animals that moved in herds, searching together for food and forming seasonal nesting colonies. Why did dinosaurs like *Hypacrosaurus* and *Triceratops* live this way? Herds offered a means of protection against roaming carnivorous dinosaurs, eager to gobble up babies and eggs.

Were dinosaurs smart?

That's a tough one. Because dinosaur brains were composed of soft tissue, none are preserved for us to study. However, paleontologists *can* measure the approximate size of dinosaurs' brains by making casts of their braincases. (It is believed that their brains did not fill the entire braincase.) Much can be learned by examining these braincases. A cast of *Tyrannosaurus rex*'s revealed that it probably had a good sense of smell. *Troodon*'s showed evidence of a large optic nerve and large eye openings, suggesting that it had keen eyesight.

But a dinosaur's braincase, or even its brain size, is not really a good way to judge intelligence. Instead, it is better to gauge "smartness" by determining an animal's ability to interact with others, sense danger, and simply survive. So how do the dinosaurs measure up in this regard? Some, like *Troodon*, probably learned quickly to live on their own, were cunning hunters, and had an excellent range of hand motion. Others, like *Maiasaura*, were able to care for their babies and likely taught their young some important survival skills.

Model of a Maiasaura *tending her nest*

Model of a Maiasaura *feeding her babies*

Were dinosaurs good parents?

Fossil records suggest that some species of dinosaurs took good care of their young. For example, tiny pieces of eggshell found in fossilized *Maiasaura* nests indicate that babies stayed there—trampling the eggshells to small bits—over the course of several weeks. Further evidence comes from finding the actual remains of baby dinosaurs in the nests; fossils indicate that their joints and bones were not well formed, which means they had to stay put. Without the ability to leave the nest, it is theorized that the adults must have brought babies the nourishment of leaves and berries. Did *Maiasaura*, aptly named the "good mother lizard," have any other maternal traits? You bet! It is believed that this species blanketed its eggs with decaying plants to keep them warm.

Like modern-day animals, however, it seems that different species provided different levels of parental care. Some dinosaurs laid their eggs and then abandoned them. Others laid their eggs in another animal's nest, abandoning any egg-tending responsibilities.

DinoChuckle!

Q. Why didn't the *Brachiosaurus* skeleton leave the museum?

A. He didn't have the guts!

TROODON EGG

MAIASAURA EGG

ORODROMEUS EGG

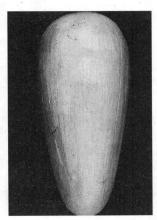

That's a Fact!

We can tell how old a tree is by counting its growth rings. Dinosaur bones have growth rings too, which paleontologists study to figure out how old they lived to be.

How old did dinosaurs live to be?

Paleontologists are not yet able to tell how old dinosaurs lived to be. But they conjecture that the dinosaurs' life spans—like those of modern-day animals—probably varied depending on the species and the environmental conditions that were present. After studying the growth rings on the inside of dinosaur bones, paleontologists estimate that some had a similar life span to humans. While many dinosaurs were fully grown after five or six years, several of these may have lived to the age of 70 or more.

Hadrosaur Femur Growth Series

Hatchling **Nestling**   **Young Adult**   **Adult**

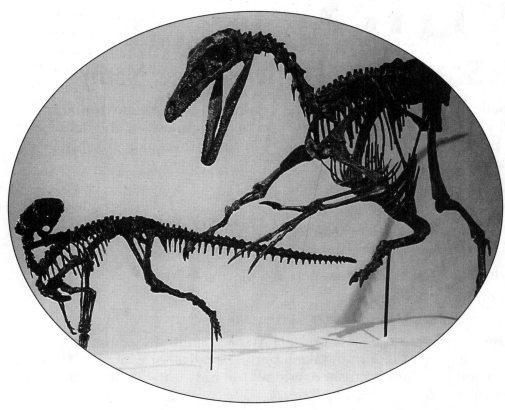

Skeletal models of a Troodon *chasing a baby* Maiasaura

Why did all dinosaurs become extinct?

The last dinosaurs died approximately 65 million years ago. Although the cause of their extinction is still a mystery, climatic change, diseases, changing plant communities, and geologic events could all have played a role.

Lately, dinosaur extinction theories have been the subject of much debate and controversy. A recent explanation, supported by many scientists, suggests that dinosaurs died out soon after a huge meteorite crashed to Earth near the Gulf of Mexico. A giant meteorite, they reason, could have landed with an impact that kicked up enough dust and debris to block out sunlight for a long time—leading to a deadly chain of events. Without the sun, all the plants died; without the plants, all the plant-eaters died; and without the plant-eaters, all the meat-eaters died. Sounds reasonable. But there is one problem with this theory: Paleontologists have not yet been able to find dinosaur skeletons in rocks dating to the period of impact. Some evidence even seems to indicate that all the dinosaurs had died *before* the meteorite hit.

What is the answer? As paleontologists search for clues to support their theories, they agree to disagree.

Where Did All the Dinos Go? Some Leading Theories:

▶ *A big meteorite crashed into Earth, changing the climatic conditions so dramatically that dinosaurs could not survive.*

▶ *Ash and gas spewing from volcanoes suffocated many of the dinosaurs.*

▶ *Diseases wiped out entire populations of dinosaurs.*

▶ *Food chain imbalances lead to the starvation of the dinosaurs.*

ACTIVITIES

Camouflage Scavenger Hunt (Science, Math)

Many paleontologists believe that dinosaurs were the same color as their environment (green and brown). Why? Because this coloration would help them escape the detection of predators, enabling the species to survive longer. To illustrate the validity of this theory, host a Camouflage Scavenger Hunt.

MATERIALS
▶three to five boxes of tricolored (red, white, green) pasta twists
▶paper cups (for collecting)

DIRECTIONS
1 Take the class outside to a large grassy area such as a playing field.

2 Toss the dried pasta all around.

3 Give kids one minute to collect as much pasta as they can.

4 When time has elapsed, return to the classroom. Have each child divide his or her pasta into red, white, and green piles, then take a personal tally. For example: *Dan—9 red, 11 white, 6 green.* When everyone's finished, add all the individual tallies to arrive at a class total. For example: *150 red, 153 white, 90 green.*

5 Invite children to explore the implications of this data by asking questions such as: Why do you think less green pasta was found than red or white? Have you ever had trouble finding something (a bug or ball) because it blended in with its environment? Do you think predatory dinosaurs would have had a harder time finding prey that was green than prey that was red? How do you think this might have helped plant-eating species to survive for millions of years?

To Extend Learning
Follow up the activity by creating a bar graph of the class's scavenger-hunt data.

Brachiosaurus Mini-Book (Language Arts)

A Day in the Life of Brachiosaurus is a mini-book for children to make and read. It humorously highlights this species' primary activity—eating! Make photo copies of page 42 and distribute one to each student.

1.

DIRECTIONS
1 Cut on the solid line (along the dinosaur's mouth) as shown in illustration 1.

Teaching Tip
If children are very young you may want to pre-cut the books, using a craft knife.

2.

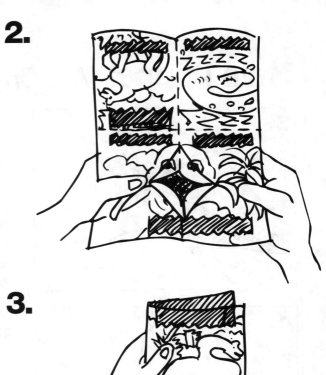

② Push the angled fold line in then out; pinching the paper on each side of the line until the mouth area sticks out as shown in illustration 2. Crease well.

③ Fold book along the dashed lines and close as shown in illustration 3

④ Demonstrate how to open and close the book so that the *Brachiosaurus* looks likes he's munching. After everyone is finished, share this fact with students: Brachiosaurus *may have eaten 600 pounds or more of plants a day!* Then read the book together! Invite prereaders to use the pictures to retell the story and fluent readers to take turns reading the story to partners.

To Extend Learning

Encourage kids to use this format as a model to create their own mini-books about meat-eating dinosaurs—*A Day in the Life of Allosaurus*—or themselves—*A Day in the Life of Shelli.*

3.

The Good Mother Peek-Through (Science)

Maiasaura means "good mother" in Greek. The species received this name because there is evidence that adults cared for their young. To learn more about this special dinosaur, make double-side photocopies of page 43–44 and distribute one to each student. Invite kids to read about *Maiasaura,* hold their papers up to the light to see the dinosaur embryos, then answer the questions on the back of the paper. Follow up the activity sheet by learning more about dinosaur parents and eggs (see page 31 for more information). If you like, compare the shape and size of a *Maiasaura* egg (8 inches long) to a chicken egg (2 inches long). Ask: Why do you think the *Maiasaura* egg is bigger than the chicken egg? What other animals can you think of that lay eggs? Make a list.

To Extend Learning

▶*Maiasaura* nests were huge—6 feet in diameter and 19 feet in circumference. To make this size concrete, represent the nest with a circle of children. Have students use a ruler to measure two 6-foot pieces of string. Crisscross the strings and tape them to the floor to make an X. Now invite your students to form a tight circle around the X: This is the size of a *Maiasaura* nest! Ask: How many children do you think will fit in the nest? Write students' predictions on the board. Then encourage volunteers, one at a time, to enter the nest. Were students correct in their estimates? Would students like to live in a *Maiasaura* nest? Why or why not?

▶Give students the opportunity to spend a little more time with this remarkable dinosaur by constructing their own *Maisaura* puppets (see the following activity).

35

Maia Puppet (Art, Creative Dramatics)

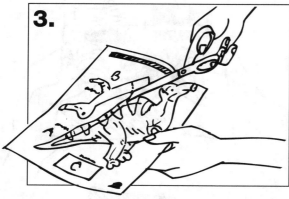

Maiasaura made Montana her home 80 million years ago, but she can make an appearance in your classroom today—in the form of this easy-to-make puppet with moveable parts.

MATERIALS

- reproducible, page 45
- oaktag
- brass fasteners
- ice-cream sticks
- crayons
- glue
- scissors
- tape

DIRECTIONS

1. Invite students to color the Maia puppet pattern. (Remind kids that since no one knows what color any of the dinosaurs were, the choice is theirs.)

2. Glue the pattern to a piece of oaktag.

3. Cut out the three parts (A, B, and C) of the puppet.

4. Use the brass fastener (or the tips of scissors) to pierce the dots on body parts A and B. Then use the fastener to attach them as shown. Fold the tab back along the dashed line.

5. Tape the pocket (part C) to the back of the puppet as shown.

6. Attach an ice-cream stick to the puppet's legs.

After kids have assembled their puppets, demonstrate how to move Maia's jaw and arm by sliding the tab back and forth inside the pocket.

To Extend Learning

After students have completed their puppets, read aloud *Maia: A Dinosaur Grows Up* by Jack Horner and James Gorman (Running Press, 1985), which tells the story of a *Maiasaura*'s life. Then, working in pairs or small groups, invite kids to use the information they learned to write short, fact-based—or funny—plays to perform with their puppets.

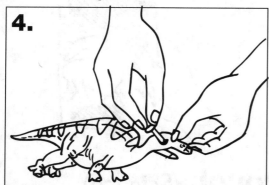

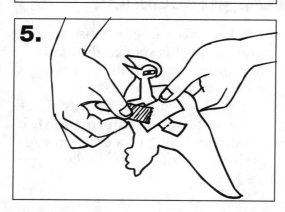

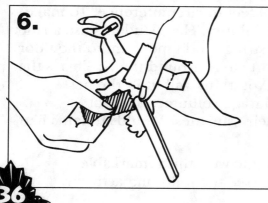

Make-and-Wear Dinosaur Crest (Art, Science)

The Hadrosaurs are famous for their incredible head ornaments called crests. Each species's crest was unique. *Corythosaurus*, for example, looked like a dinner plate set on its edge and *Parasaurolophus*'s was tubular, beginning at its nose and extending over its head—sometimes growing to lengths of 6 feet! Learn more about this fascinating group of dinosaurs, then give your students the opportunity to create their own *Parasaurolophus* crest.

MATERIALS
▶ reproducible, page 46   ▶ oaktag   ▶ crayons or markers   ▶ glue and tape

DIRECTIONS

1 Reproduce the crest pattern and headband on page 46, and distributing one to each student.

2 Cut out the two pieces band and paste or tape the ends together to form one long strip. Have each child wrap the strip around his or her head and tape it at the appropriate length.

3 Cut the crest pattern and use it as a guide to trace two identical pieces on heavy oak tag. Cut them out and paste them together as shown, being careful not to paste the tab.

4 Invite kids to decorate their crests with crayons or markers. Remind them that no one knows what color any of the dinosaurs were, so they should let their imaginations go!

5 Insert the cut in the crest over the band. Open the flaps and tape to the inside of the band as shown. Now kids are ready to become *Parasaurolophuses!*

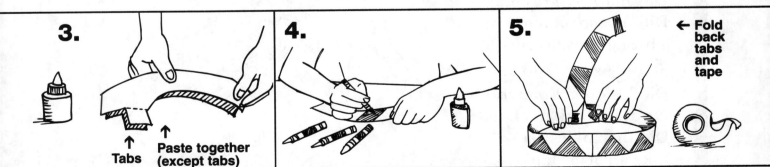

3. ↑ Tabs ↑ Paste together (except tabs)

4.

5. ← Fold back tabs and tape

To Extend Learning
After constructing the dinosaur crests, research *Parasaurolophus* and share some leading theories about the purpose of its crest. Here are a few:

▶ The crest allowed the species to identify its own.

▶ The crest enhanced the species's sense of smell.

▶ The crest enabled the species to make distinctive noises.

Invite children to build critical-thinking skills by asking: What do you think the crest was used for? Welcome innovative theories. If you like, publish children's responses on a piece of chart paper. For another idea, try "DinoSounds," which follows.

Dinosounds (Language Arts)

Was the world of dinosaurs silent or was it full of rich and unusual sounds? We may never know for certain. But most paleontologists conjecture that dinosaurs were able to make an array of noises—intended to scare off predators or call other members of their species. These sounds may have included: bellows, honks, moos, squeaks, roars, snarls, snorts, grunts, hisses, rumbles, and hoots to name just a few.

Share the following poem with students by reading it aloud or copying it onto a piece of chart paper to recite chorally.

Dinosaur Dins

Did *Stegosaurus* bellow like
A longhorn steer in Texas?
Could a songbird's tweet
Or twitter beat
Tyrannosaurus rex's?

Did *Pterodactyl* cackle?
Did *Brachiosaurus* bray?
Did *Monoclonius* toot
Through his horny snoot
Ta ra ra boom de ay?

Did little *Lambeosaurus* baa
Or did it bark in chorus?
Did the ankles clank
Like an army tank
On an *Ankylosaurus?*

Today cars, planes, subway trains
Raise a whole lot of hullaballoo
But the rumble and roar
Of a dinosaur
I haven't heard—have you?

by X.J. Kennedy

To Extend Learning

After reading the poem, ask: What sounds do you think dinosaurs made? Then build critical-thinking skills by inviting students to invent that noise. Give kids five minutes or so to practice and perfect their sounds quietly, then present them to the rest of the class. If you like, record the noises on a tape recorder and present a Dino Sound Award to the creator of the class's very favorite. After everyone's had a chance to perform, give kids a few minutes to become dinosaurs by moving around the room on two or four legs while making their sounds and wearing their crests.

Late Cretaceous Food Pyramid (Science)

Give kids the opportunity to explore a dinosaur ecosystem by constructing a Late Cretaceous Food Pyramid. Reproduce and distribute copies of page 47 to students. Have each child cut out the cards along the dashed lines. Then challenge them to place the meat-eater, the plant-eaters, and the plants in the correct categories. (If children are having trouble distinguishing the meat-eater from plant-eaters, encourage them to refer to their Dinosaur Identification Cards or a dinosaur encyclopedia.) When kids are finished constructing their pyramids, invite them to discuss this Dino-Challenge—*If all the plants died, what would happen to the dinosaurs?*—with a friend and respond on another sheet of paper or in their journals.

If students are very young, you might get them thinking along the right track by posing questions such as: Why do you think there are more plants than plant-eaters? More plant-eaters than meat-eaters? What would happen if all the plants died? What would happen if all the plant-eaters died? Which of these plants and species are still around today? If you like, research some dinosaurs that paleontologists believe may have been omnivores (both plant- and meat-eaters), such as *Ornithomimus*.

To Extend Learning

▶ Research other dinosaur-era plants, plant-eaters, and meat-eaters. Use the information to make a giant food pyramid modeled on this one.

▶ Make a Foods People Eat chart by brainstorming two lists: *Foods we eat that are plants* and *Foods we eat that are meats*. Publish the information in the form of a big book.

Extinction Cartoon Strip
(Reflective Thinking)

There are almost as many extinction theories as there are paleontologists. Introduce your students to some of the leading hypotheses (see page 33), then reinforce the most popular one—that a meteorite crashed to Earth—with this cartoon-sequencing activity. Photocopy and distribute page 48 to each child. Challenge kids to cut out the cartoon squares, put them in order, then paste them in place. When everyone is finished, read the cartoon strip together. What do kids think of this theory? Do they agree with it? Why or why not?

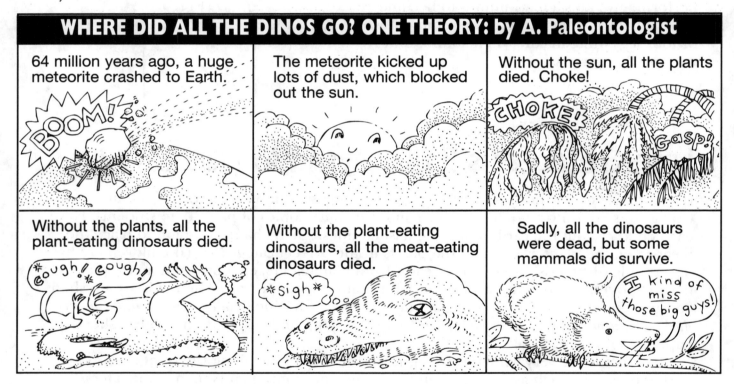

WHERE DID ALL THE DINOS GO? ONE THEORY: by A. Paleontologist

64 million years ago, a huge meteorite crashed to Earth.
BOOM!

The meteorite kicked up lots of dust, which blocked out the sun.

Without the sun, all the plants died. Choke!
CHOKE! Gasp!

Without the plants, all the plant-eating dinosaurs died.
Cough! Cough!

Without the plant-eating dinosaurs, all the meat-eating dinosaurs died.
Sigh

Sadly, all the dinosaurs were dead, but some mammals did survive.
I kind of miss those big guys!

To Extend Learning

▶ Encourage students to research this and other dinosaur extinction theories in greater depth and/or to develop a theory of their own. Then invite students to present and support their theories by creating their own cartoon strips. When everyone is finished, ask kids to share their creations with the class. If you like, take a poll to find out which is the number-one extinction theory!

▶ Demonstrate how lack of sun can have a disastrous effect on plants with the activity that follows.

Plants Minus Sun (Science)

Two imperative parts of an ecosystem—including the dinosaurs'—were plants and the sun—without them, the food chain would collapse. Here's a simple science experiment to demonstrate what happens to plants without the warm, nurturing rays of the sun.

MATERIALS

▶ 2 small houseplants that are the same type and size

▶ A cardboard box big enough to hold one of the plants

DIRECTIONS

1 Water both plants.

2 Put one inside the box and seal it so that no light seeps in.

3 Place the plant and the boxed plant near a window.

4 Four or five days later, open the box and take out the plant. What happened to the plant in the box? Invite students to tell you why they think the boxed plant became wilted and sick. Guide children to understand that plants need the sun to survive. Then encourage them to think about how the absence of sun could have an impact on the dinosaurs, and eventually bring about their extinction.

To Extend Learning

Follow up the experiment by asking: Do people need the sun too? Why or why not? Brainstorm a list of everything that needs the sun. Are there any living things that don't need the sun—either directly or indirectly—to survive?

Then he'd stomp and chomp and eat and eat—
pine needles in trees and ferns at his feet.

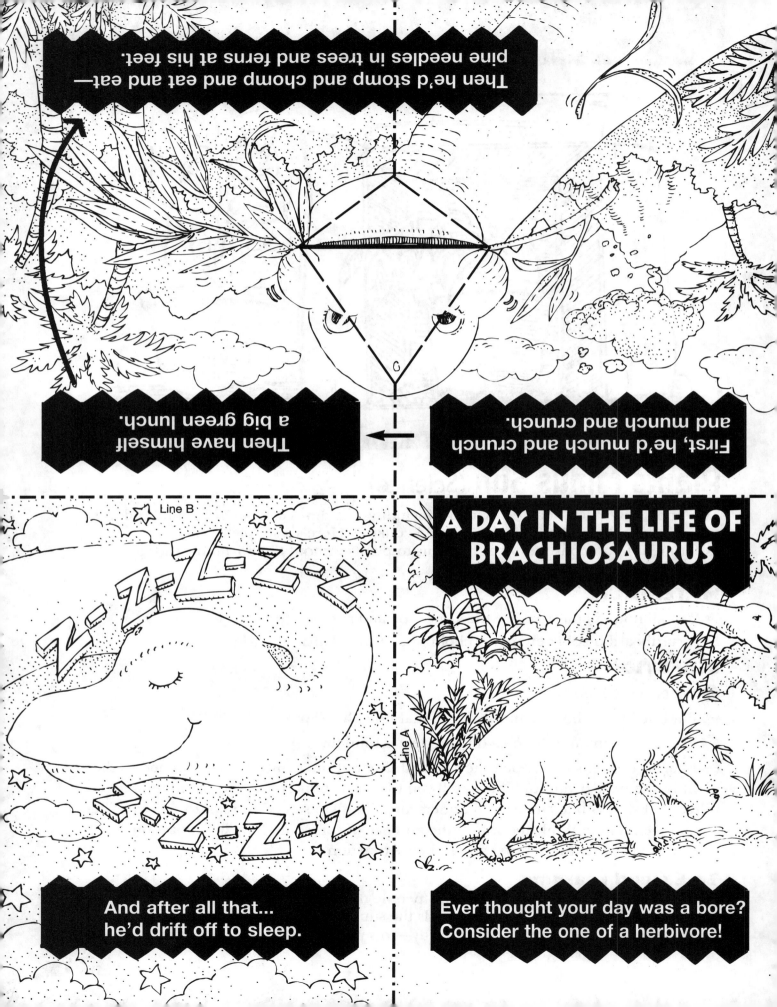

Then have himself
a big green lunch.

First, he'd munch and crunch
and munch and crunch.

Line B

And after all that...
he'd drift off to sleep.

A DAY IN THE LIFE OF BRACHIOSAURUS

Line A

Ever thought your day was a bore?
Consider the one of a herbivore!

The Good Mother

Maiasaura is called the "good mother lizard" because she took great care of her babies before and after they were hatched. Here is her nest. Hold your paper up to the light to see what's inside the eggs. Then turn your paper over and answer the questions on the back.

1 What's inside the eggs?_____

2 How many eggs are in the nest?_____

3 This *Maiasaura* mom weighs more than a car. What do you think might happen if she sat on her tiny eggs?_____

_____

4 If a *Maiasaura* mom couldn't sit on her eggs, how do you think she kept them warm at night? Hint: Turn this paper over and look at what's covering them.

_____

_____

5 What other animals can you think of that lay eggs?_____

_____

DINO-CHALLENGE: Make up a math problem about a nest of *Maiasaura* eggs. Write it down, then share it with a friend.

Embryo

Shell

Maia Puppet

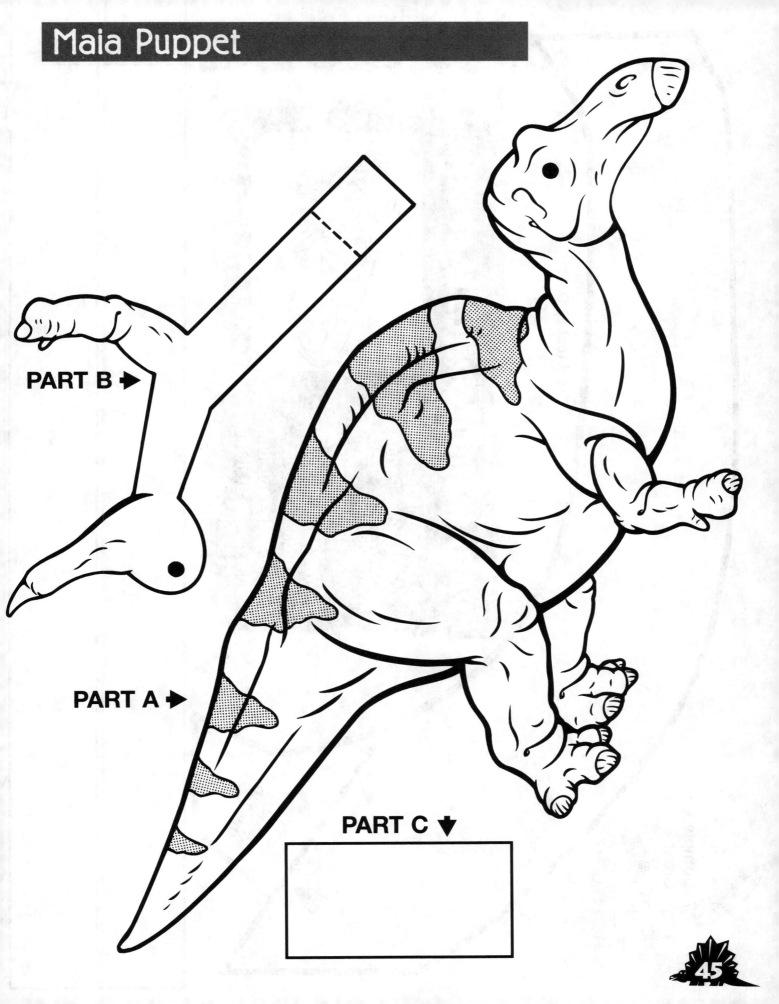

PART B ➤

PART A ➤

PART C ▼

paste

Crest (cut 2)

PARASAUROLOPHUS FACT BOX

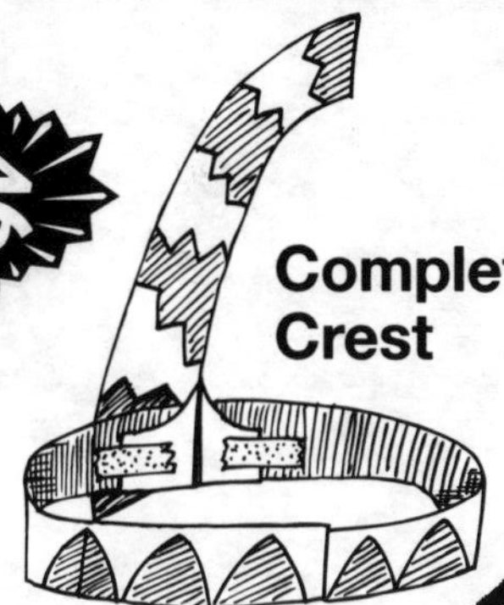

▶ Lived during the late Cretaceous Period

▶ Ate plants

▶ Walked on two legs

▶ Was a member of the Hadrosaur group

▶ Had a six-foot-long crest that began at its nose

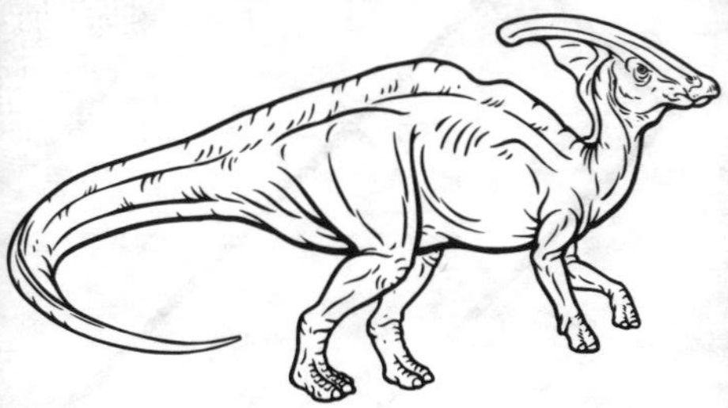

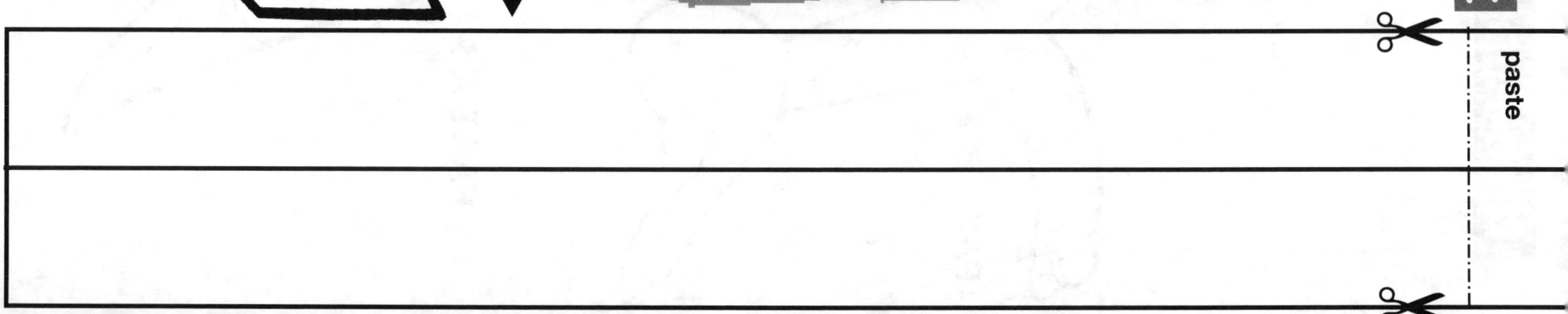

Band

fold

cut

Don't paste this tab

Completed Crest

Late Cretaceous Food Pyramid

Cut out the cards and paste them where they go.

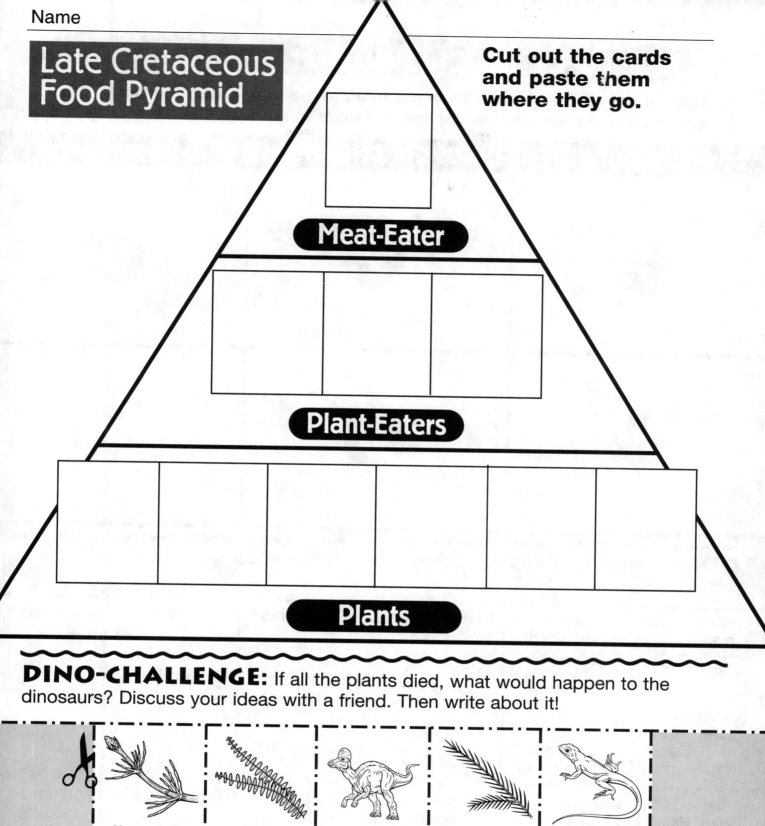

Meat-Eater

Plant-Eaters

Plants

DINO-CHALLENGE: If all the plants died, what would happen to the dinosaurs? Discuss your ideas with a friend. Then write about it!

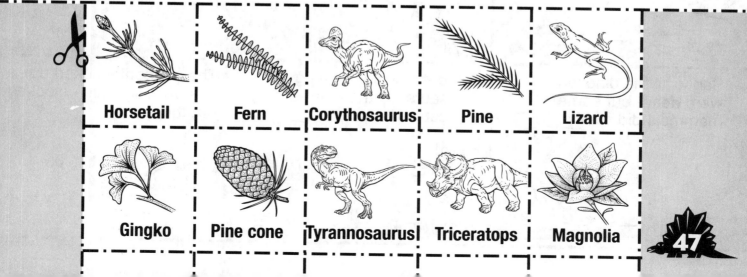

Horsetail | Fern | Corythosaurus | Pine | Lizard

Gingko | Pine cone | Tyrannosaurus | Triceratops | Magnolia

47

Name

Extinction Cartoon Strip

Cut out the cartoon boxes. Then put them in the right order to make a comic strip that tells one of the most popular extinction theories.

WHERE DID ALL THE DINOS GO? ONE THEORY: by A. Paleontologist

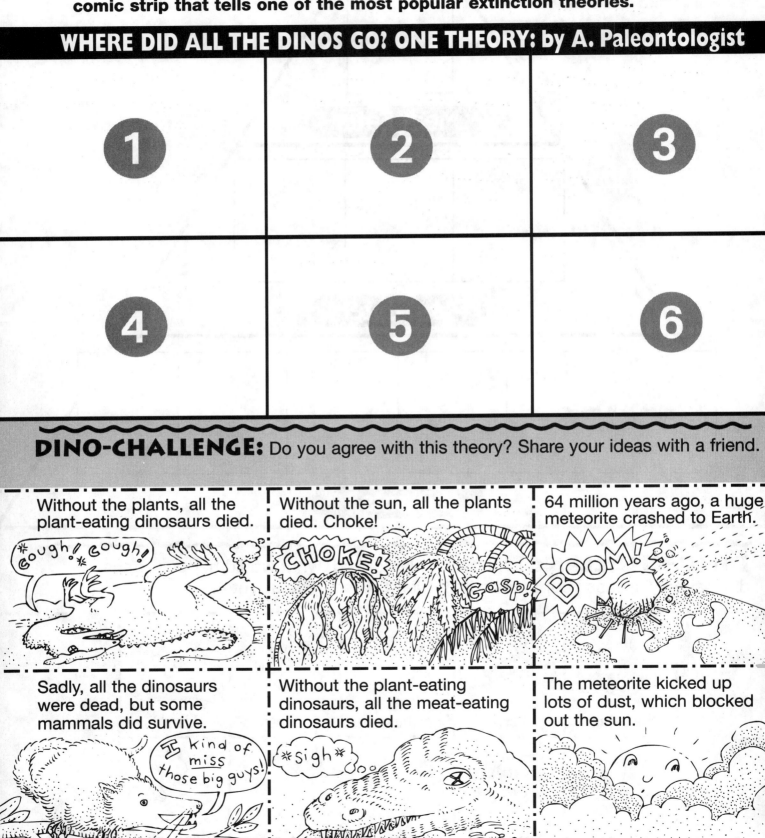

1	**2**	**3**
4	**5**	**6**

DINO-CHALLENGE: Do you agree with this theory? Share your ideas with a friend.

Without the plants, all the plant-eating dinosaurs died.

Cough! Cough!

Without the sun, all the plants died. Choke!

CHOKE! Gasp!

64 million years ago, a huge meteorite crashed to Earth.

BOOM!

Sadly, all the dinosaurs were dead, but some mammals did survive.

I kind of miss those big guys!

Without the plant-eating dinosaurs, all the meat-eating dinosaurs died.

sigh

The meteorite kicked up lots of dust, which blocked out the sun.

"MEET" THE SPECIES

How are dinosaurs classified?

In order to communicate with one another and show relationships between different kinds of organisms, some biologists and paleontologists group dinosaurs—and other animals—together using a system of classification called *cladistics*. Cladistics is based on the idea that the more characteristics animals share, the more *closely* related they are to one another. Scientists look for features that separate groups of animals, or individual animals, from all others. For example, key features found in all dinosaurs' hip joints, femurs, knees, and ankle joints separate dinosaurs from other archosaurs, such as crocodiles and pterosaurus. Dinosaurs can be further divided into smaller groups by defining the features they have in common. Each group of dinosaurs with shared features is called a *clade*. Clades vary in size: Some consist of many species while others are made up of only one.

Jack Horner with a T. rex *skull*

Classifying Dinosaurs

Order: Ornithischian

Their hip bones look like this:

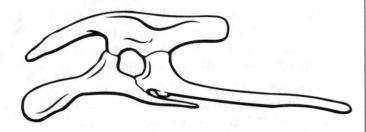

MAIN GROUPS:

Ornithopods
CHARACTERISTICS: herbivorous, bipedal, toothless beaks
EXAMPLES: *Iguanodon, Maiasaura*

Ceratopsians
CHARACTERISTICS: herbivorous, adorned with horns or frills
EXAMPLES: *Triceratops, Centrosaurus*

Ankylosaurs
CHARACTERISTICS: herbivorous, quadropedal, with spikes and armor
EXAMPLES: *Euoplocephalus, Nodosaurus*

Pachycephalosaurs
CHARACTERISTICS: herbivorous, bipedal, with thick bony skulls
EXAMPLES: *Stegoceras, Pachycephalosaurus*

Stegosaurs
CHARACTERISTICS: herbivorous, quadrapedal, with plates or spikes on their back
EXAMPLES: *Kentrosaurus, Stegosaurus*

Order: Saurischian

Their hip bones look like this:

MAIN GROUPS:

Sauropods
CHARACTERISTICS: herbivorous, large in size, quadrapedal, long necks, long tails
EXAMPLES: *Seismosaurus, Brachiosaurus*

Theropods
CHARACTERISTICS: carnivorous, bipedal, sharp claws
EXAMPLES: *Allosaurus, Tyrannosaurus*

Dino Chuckle!

Q. Why did *Allosaurus* chase his tail?

A. He was trying to make ends meet.

How many species were there?

A lot! About a thousand species of dinosaurs have been discovered to date, with new ones being unearthed every year. In fact, it has been estimated that fewer than one percent of all the species that ever lived have been discovered and described so far.

DINOSAUR HALL OF FAME

First

The earliest-known dinosaur is *Staurikosaurus* who may have lived in the middle Triassic Period.

Biggest

Adult *Seismosaurus* have been measured at 120 feet long.

Smallest

Compsognathus was about the size of a chicken.

Fastest

Troodon may have run as fast as 30 miles per hour.

Longest Claw

Therizinosaurus had claws that were up to 28 inches long. Yikes!

Longest Teeth

Both *Tyrannosaurus rex* and *Tarbosaurus* had 6-inch-long teeth.

Most Teeth

Anatosaurus had as many as 1,600 teeth (but not all of them were being used at the same time).

Fewest Teeth

Ornithomimus had no teeth at all.

Ugliest

Many agree that *Pachycephalasaurus*, whose head was covered with spikes and warts, was the homliest of all.

Biggest Eggs

Dinosaur eggs the size of basketballs have been found. Unfortunately, we don't yet know which species they belonged to.

ACTIVITIES

COMPSOGNATHUS
(komp-sug-NAY-thus)

Name means: pretty jaw
Bones found in: France, Germany
Lived during: Jurassic Period
Became extinct: 140 million years ago
Ate: meat   **Walked on:** two legs
Measured: 3 feet   **Weighed:** 6 lbs.

FAST FACTS:
➤ *Compsognathus* was one of the smallest dinosaurs. It was about the size of a chicken.
➤ *Compsognathus* feasted ~~on~~ ~~nasty~~ things like insects and lizards.

Back

Front

Dinosaur Identification Cards (Science, Art)

The Dinosaur Identification Cards on pages 57 to 62 will help your students become familiar with 12 of the most popular species. Reproduce these pages. Then have students cut out the cards along the solid lines, fold the cards along the dashed lines, and paste them together. Invite kids to use the cards with some or all of the activities below. If you like, encourage students to invent their own games or to create new cards focusing on other species that intrigue them.

A Question of Color (Reflective Thinking)

No dinosaur skin has ever been found, which means that no one knows for sure what color any of the dinosaurs were. Paleontologists *do* have a lot of theories, of course (see page 24 for some of these). Share and discuss their ideas with students. Then challenge kids to color their ID cards based on one of these theories or on a theory of their own.

To Extend Learning

▶ To demonstrate the validity of the popular notion that dinosaurs were shades of green and grey, follow up the activity with "Camouflage Scavenger Hunt" (see page 34).

▶ Encourage students to write a paragraph or two explaining their color choice and to share their expository writing with the rest of the class. What does the class think is the best theory? Take a poll!

Sorting Out Dinosaurs (Math)

This activity is designed to help students build sorting skills as they learn about specific dinosaurs. Reproduce pages 63 and 64 and distribute them to each student (or children can work with partners). Invite kids to fill in the chart, using the information on their ID cards. For example, in #1, students should sort their cards into two stacks: Dinosaurs whose bones have been found in the United States and Dinosaurs whose bones have not been found in the United States. Next, students should count the cards in each stack, record the number in the dinosaur shape, then use the data to write a dinosaur fact. For example, in #1, they might write: "Most of these dinosaurs had bones found in the United States."

To Extend Learning

After they've completed the chart, challenge students to invent new ways to sort their cards. For example: Dinosaurs that weighed more than I do and Dinosaurs that weighed less than I do.

Dinosaur Match-Up (Science)

Here's a *dino*-mite way to fill those extra minutes in the morning or just before the bell rings. Ask children to lay their 12 ID cards, picture-side up, on their desks. Then write the name of one of the dinosaurs—*Coelophysis*, for example—on the board. Now challenge students to turn over the dinosaur picture they think is *Coelophysis*. If kids get it right on their first try, they keep the card. If kids get it wrong, they put the incorrect card back, picture-side up, on their desk. In each subsequent round, write the name of a new dinosaur on the board and have students make their best guess. After all 12 dinosaur names have been written on the board, ask students to tally their scores by giving themselves a point for each dinosaur they correctly identified on the first try. The child with the most points wins!

To Extend Learning

After play, invite students to discuss their strategies for identifying the dinosaurs. Were some easier to remember than others? Why?

Dueling Dinosaurs (Reflective Thinking)

This simple game is modeled on the classic card game War. Have each child choose a partner. Each partner shuffles his or her 12 ID cards and puts them in a stack, picture-side up. Next, players agree on one of these criterion for the round: weighs more, weighs less, is longer, is shorter, became extinct earlier, became extinct later. Let's say they choose weighs more. Now they both turn over their top dinosaur cards to reveal the dinosaurs' weights. The child with the card bearing the heavier dinosaur collects the other player's card. (If the dinosaurs weigh the same amount, each player keeps his or her own card.) After players have dueled with each of their 12 cards, they count their spoils. The player with the most cards wins. If students like, they can play another round with a different criterion. Cards are returned to their owners when the game is over.

T. Rex Challenge (Reflective Thinking)

Point out this interesting Fast Fact on the *Tyrannosaurus rex* ID card: T. rex's *arms were so tiny that it couldn't even scratch its chin.* In fact, paleontologists aren't sure how this species used its two-clawed arms. What do your students think? Invite them to look at the picture of *T. rex* , then complete this sentence: *I think* T. rex *used its tiny arms to* _____.
Compile the responses on a piece of chart paper. (Welcome innovative ideas.) If you like, have kids brainstorm a list of things they use *their* arms for. Hang the charts around the room to enjoy throughout your dinosaur unit.

Sizing Up Dinosaurs (Math)

In the activity on pages 65 and 66, your students will create a bar graph to compare the lengths of the 12 dinosaurs on their ID cards. Reproduce both pages and distribute a copy to each child. Then invite students to find each dinosaur's length and record it on the graph by shading the appropriate number of rectangular boxes. For example,

Brachiosaurus is 75 feet long so kids would shade up to box 75. If you like, have children use a different color crayon for each dinosaur; this will make the information a bit easier to read. After students are finished, challenge them to use their graphs to answer the related questions.

To Extend Learning

To give kids a concrete sense of the length of these dinosaurs, followup this activity sheet with "Body-saurus" or "Life-Size *Velociraptor* Puzzle" which follows.

Body-saurus (Math)

Kids will learn from their ID cards that a *Brachiosaurus* was 75 feet from its head to its tail—but just how long is 75 feet? Help students visualize this impressive measurement by creating a Body-saurus.

MATERIALS

▶ tape measure or yardstick   ▶ string   ▶ tape or stakes

DIRECTIONS

1 Pick one of the dinosaurs from the cards. Write its name and length on the board. For example: *Brachiosaurus, 75 feet.* Ask students to imagine just how long that is.

2 Take kids to a grassy playing field (or the gym), and with the aid of a tape measure or yardstick, measure 75 feet of string from a roll. Spread the string out in a straight line, staking (or taping) each end. This is the length of your dinosaur.

3 After kids have oohed and aahed over the incredible length of this species, divide the class into cooperative groups of four or five. Challenge each group to work collectively to answer this question: How many students, lying head to foot will it take to equal the length of a *Brachiosaurus?* After each group has made a thoughtful guess, invite students to lie down and see which was the closest. Would this dinosaur fit in their classroom?

To Extend Learning

Back in the classroom, invite groups to represent the weights of some of the dinosaurs on their ID cards, using this formula: 1 dried bean (or paper clip or connecting bead) = 1,000 pounds. Have kids count out the correct number of manipulatives for each species, put them in a pile, and label it with the appropriate ID card. Use the piles to build estimation skills by asking questions such as: Is *Brachiosaurus*'s weight closer to *Tyrannosaurus* or *Troodon*? Which dinosaurs weigh the same amount?

Life-Size Velociraptor Puzzle (Science, Art)

This cooperative activity gives students the opportunity to spend a little extra time with one of their favorite dinosaurs—*Velociraptor!*

MATERIALS

▶ reproducible page 67   ▶ 8½-by-11-inch paper   ▶ pencils

DIRECTIONS

1 Photocopy page 67. Cut the picture apart along the solid lines to make rectangular puzzle pieces. If your students like surprises, don't tell them what the image is!

2 Give a puzzle piece and a sheet of paper to each student. Make sure all 30 pieces are distributed. (If there are less than 30 children, give some students two puzzle pieces and two pieces of paper.)

3 Challenge each student to use a pencil to enlarge the puzzle piece's image on the $8\frac{1}{2}$-by-11-inch paper. Stress that kids should be as accurate as possible. As students are working, circulate around the room to make sure they've all copied the image *exactly*. When everyone's finished, have each student write the puzzle piece's number on the back of the $8\frac{1}{2}$-by-11-inch paper.

4 Now you are ready to assemble the puzzle. Clear a large floor space (at least 4-by-6 feet) and put the pieces together in numerical order. Go from left to right, laying six papers horizontally and five papers vertically, as illustrated above. If you didn't tell kids what the image was, encourage them to predict what kind of dinosaur is emerging.

After the puzzle is complete, tape it together and invite kids to measure the dinosaur and compare its size with their own. Color, then hang the *Velociraptor* in the classroom to be enjoyed throughout your dinosaur unit.

Which Dinosaur am I? Guessing Game
(Reflective Thinking)

After kids are very familiar with the 12 dinosaurs on their ID cards, build their critical-thinking skills with this challenging guessing game. To prepare, tape a dinosaur ID card to each child's back with the information side facing out. (Make sure they don't see the card you've chosen for them; the information is for the others students to read.)

55

Next, invite kids to mingle around the room and ask others yes-or-no questions about their dinosaur identity, such as: Am I a meat-eater? Do I walk on two legs? Did I live during the Cretaceous Period? When students think they know their identity, they can approach you with their guesses. If they are correct—they win!—ask them to sit down. If they are incorrect, have them continue their questioning, returning to you when they have a new guess. Play until all students have guessed their identities. Then celebrate with a huge round of applause befitting these wonderful beasts!

Dinosaur Wheel of Fame (Science)

Which dinosaur was the biggest? the smallest? the fastest? Invite students to "meet" some of the most infamous species by constructing a Dinosaur Wheel of Fame. Make photocopies of page 68 and distribute one to each student. Ask kids to cut out the wheels along the dashed lines, place wheel A on top of wheel B, then poke a brass fastener through the dot to attach them. If they like, children can decorate their wheels using crayons or markers. As kids turn the wheels, they'll find out some exciting facts, which they can share with their family and friends.

To Extend Learning

Follow up the activity by researching other dinosaurs to go in a class Dinosaur Hall of Fame. Include objective and/or subjective picks, such as the earliest, last, or fiercest dinosaur. If you like, make fancy ribbons or medallions to award to these special species. See page 51 for some memorable dinosaurs to include.

Dinosaur Identification Cards

The cards on these six pages will help you learn more about some of the dinosaurs. To make the cards, cut along the solid lines. Then fold along the dashed lines. Tape or paste the front and back of each card together.

BRACHIOSAURUS (BRAK-ee-uh-SAWR-us)

Name means: arm lizard
Bones found in: Tanzania, United States
Lived during: Jurassic Period
Became extinct: 145 million years ago
Ate: plants **Walked on:** four legs
Measured: 75 feet **Weighed:** 150,000 lbs.

FAST FACTS:

▶ *Brachiosaurus* was one of the biggest dinosaurs. He weighed as much as 15 elephants and stood as tall as a four-story building.

▶ *Brachiosaurus's* nostrils were on top of its head.

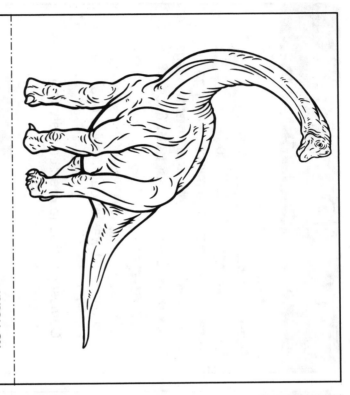

COELOPHYSIS (see-lo-FISE-us)

Name means: hollow form
Bones found in: United States
Lived during: Triassic Period
Became extinct: 202 million years ago
Ate: meat **Walked on:** two legs
Measured: 10 feet **Weighed:** 65 lbs.

FAST FACTS:

▶ *Coelophysis* was one of the very first dinosaurs.

▶ *Coelophysis* was a meat-eater whose diet may have included its own babies!

COMPSOGNATHUS (komp-sug-NAY-thus)

Name means: pretty jaw
Bones found in: France, Germany
Lived during: Jurassic Period
Became extinct: 140 million years ago
Ate: meat   **Walked on:** two legs
Measured: 3 feet   **Weighed:** 6 lbs.

FAST FACTS:

▶ *Compsognathus* was one of the smallest dinosaurs. It was about the size of a chicken.

▶ *Compsognathus* feasted on tasty things like insects and lizards.

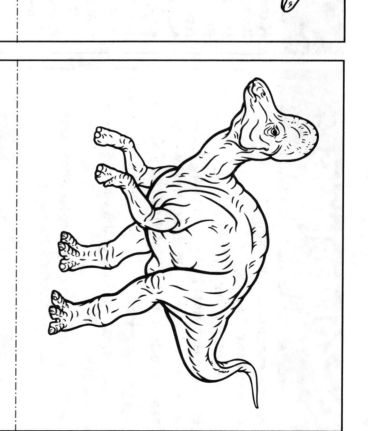

CORYTHOSAURUS (ko-RITH-uh-SAWR-us)

Name means: helmet lizard
Bones found in: Canada
Lived during: Cretaceous Period
Became extinct: 72 million years ago
Ate: plants   **Walked on:** four legs
Measured: 30 feet   **Weighed:** 6,000 lbs.

FAST FACTS:

▶ *Corythosaurus* had a huge bump on its head, which looked like a dinner plate set on its edge. This is called a crest.

▶ *Corythosaurus* had pebbly skin that was the texture of a football.

IGUANODON
(i-GUA-no-DON)

Name means: iguana tooth
Bones found in: Belgium, England, Germany, Mongolia, Tunisia, United States
Lived during: Cretaceous Period
Became extinct: 110 million years ago
Ate: plants   **Walked on:** two or four legs
Measured: 30 feet   **Weighed:** 10,000 lbs.

FAST FACTS:

► *Iguanodon* was one of the first dinosaurs to be discovered. In 1821, Mary Anne Mantell found its teeth while rock hunting.

► *Iguanodon* had a spike for a thumb, which was probably used to jab enemies.

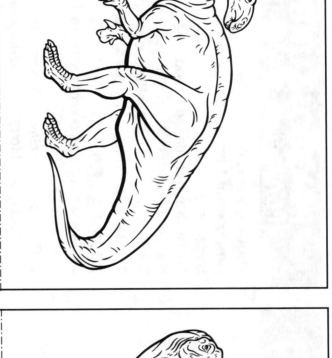

MAIASAURA
(my-uh-SAWR-a)

Name means: good mother lizard
Bones found in: United States
Lived during: Cretaceous Period
Became extinct: 73 million years ago
Ate: plants   **Walked on:** two legs
Measured: 30 feet   **Weighed:** 6,000 lbs.

FAST FACTS:

► Mother *Maiasaura* laid eggs and probably took care of their babies in the nest.

► Scientists think that *Maiasaura* lived in herds and migrated.

PLATEOSAURUS
(PLAT-ee-oh-SAWR-us)

Name means: flat lizard
Bones found in: France, Germany, Switzerland
Lived during: Triassic Period
Became extinct: 210 million years ago
Ate: plants **Walked on:** two legs
Measured: 25 feet **Weighed:** 3,000 lbs.

FAST FACTS:

▶ *Plateosaurus* was one of the earliest dinosaurs.

▶ *Plateosaurus's* clawed fingers were probably used to rake up plants to eat.

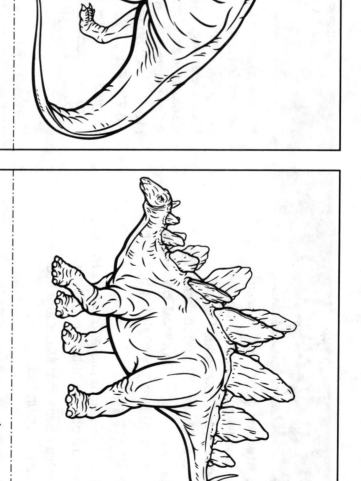

STEGOSAURUS
(STEG-uh-SAWR-us)

Name means: roof lizard
Bones found in: United States
Lived during: Jurassic Period
Became extinct: 145 million years ago
Ate: plants **Walked on:** two or four legs
Measured: 30 feet **Weighed:** 4,000 lbs.

FAST FACTS:

▶ *Stegosaurus's* brain was only the size of a walnut.

▶ *Stegosaurus's* diamond-shaped plates may have been used to absorb sunlight to help to keep him warm.

TRICERATOPS (try-SAIR-uh-tops)

Name means: three-horned face
Bones found in: Canada, United States
Lived during: Cretaceous Period
Became extinct: 65 million years ago
Ate: plants　　**Walked on:** four legs
Measured: 30 feet　**Weighed:** 16,000 lbs.

FAST FACTS:

▶ *Triceratops* had a beak like a turtle and sharp teeth that cut through leaves like a pair of scissors.

▶ *Triceratops* probably used its three sharp horns to attract female dinosaurs and defend itself.

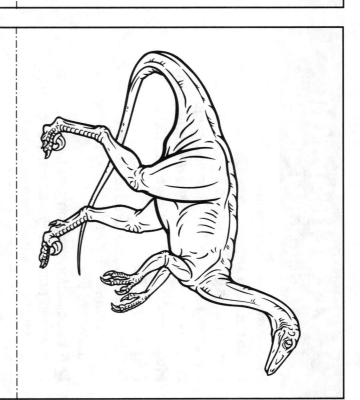

TROODON (true-OH-don)

Name means: wound tooth
Bones found in: Canada, United States
Lived during: Cretaceous Period
Became extinct: 70 million years ago
Ate: meat　　**Walked on:** two legs
Measured: 5 feet　**Weighed:** 50 lbs.

FAST FACTS:

▶ *Troodon* had a very large brain and may have been the smartest dinosaur.

▶ *Troodon* probably ate other species' eggs and babies.

TYRANNOSAURUS (tye-RAN-uh-SAWR-us)

Name means: tyrant lizard
Bones found in: Canada, United States
Lived during: Cretaceous Period
Became extinct: 65 million years ago
Ate: meat   **Walked on:** two legs
Measured: 45 feet   **Weighed:** 14,000 lbs.

FAST FACTS:

▶ *Tyrannosaurus'* arms were so tiny he couldn't even scratch his chin.

▶ *Tyrannosaurus'* 60 razor-sharp teeth were the size of steak-knives.

VELOCIRAPTOR (vel-o-si-RAP-tor)

Name means: fast predator
Bones found in: Mongolia, China
Lived during: Cretaceous Period
Became extinct: 70 million years ago
Ate: meat   **Walked on:** two legs
Measured: 6 feet   **Weighed:** 150 lbs.

FAST FACTS:

▶ Fierce *Velociraptor* used its sharp teeth and clawed hands and feet to attack dinosaurs twice its size.

▶ A *Velociraptor* skeleton was found wrapped around a *Protoceratops* skeleton. Scientists think they died while fighting.

Name

Sorting Out Dinosaurs

To answer each question, sort your Dinosaur ID cards into two stacks. Then use that information to write a fact. We filled in the first one for you.

Dinosaurs whose bones have been found in the United States:

Dinosaurs whose bones have not been found in the United States:

FACT 1:

Most of these dinosaurs had bones that were found in the United States.

Dinosaurs that ate plants:

Dinosaurs that ate meat:

FACT 2:

Dinosaurs that were less than 20 feet long:

Dinosaurs that were more than 20 feet long:

FACT 3:

DINO-CHALLENGE: Can you think of some more ways to sort your Dinosaur ID Cards? Share them with a friend!

Sorting Out Dinosaurs (Part Two)

Now fill in this chart. To do these sorts, you'll need to divide your dinosaur cards into three stacks.

Dinosaurs that walked on two legs:

Dinosaurs that walked on four legs:

Dinosaurs that walked on two or four legs:

FACT 4:

Dinosaurs that lived during the Triassic Period:

Dinosaurs that lived during the Jurassic Period:

Dinosaurs that lived during the Cretaceous Period:

FACT 5:

Name _____

Sizing Up Dinosaurs

Use the information on your dinosaur cards to graph the lengths of each of the 12 dinosaurs. Then use the graph to answer these questions.

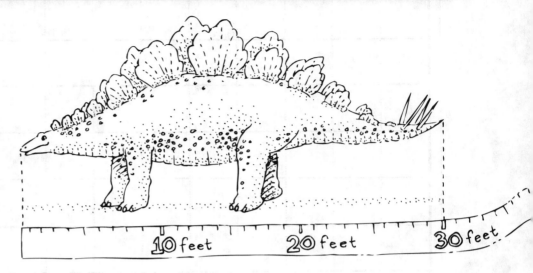

10 feet   20 feet   30 feet

1 Which dinosaur is the longest?

_____

2 Which dinosaur is the shortest?

_____

3 How many dinosaurs are longer than a school bus?

_____

4 How many dinosaurs are shorter than a school bus?

_____

5 What length are most of the dinosaurs?

_____

6 How many feet longer is *Corythosaurus* than *Coelophysis*?

_____

~~~~~~

DINO-CHALLENGE: Write your own question. Then use the graph to answer it.

7 _____

_____

Sizing Up Dinosaurs (Continued)

Name ____________________

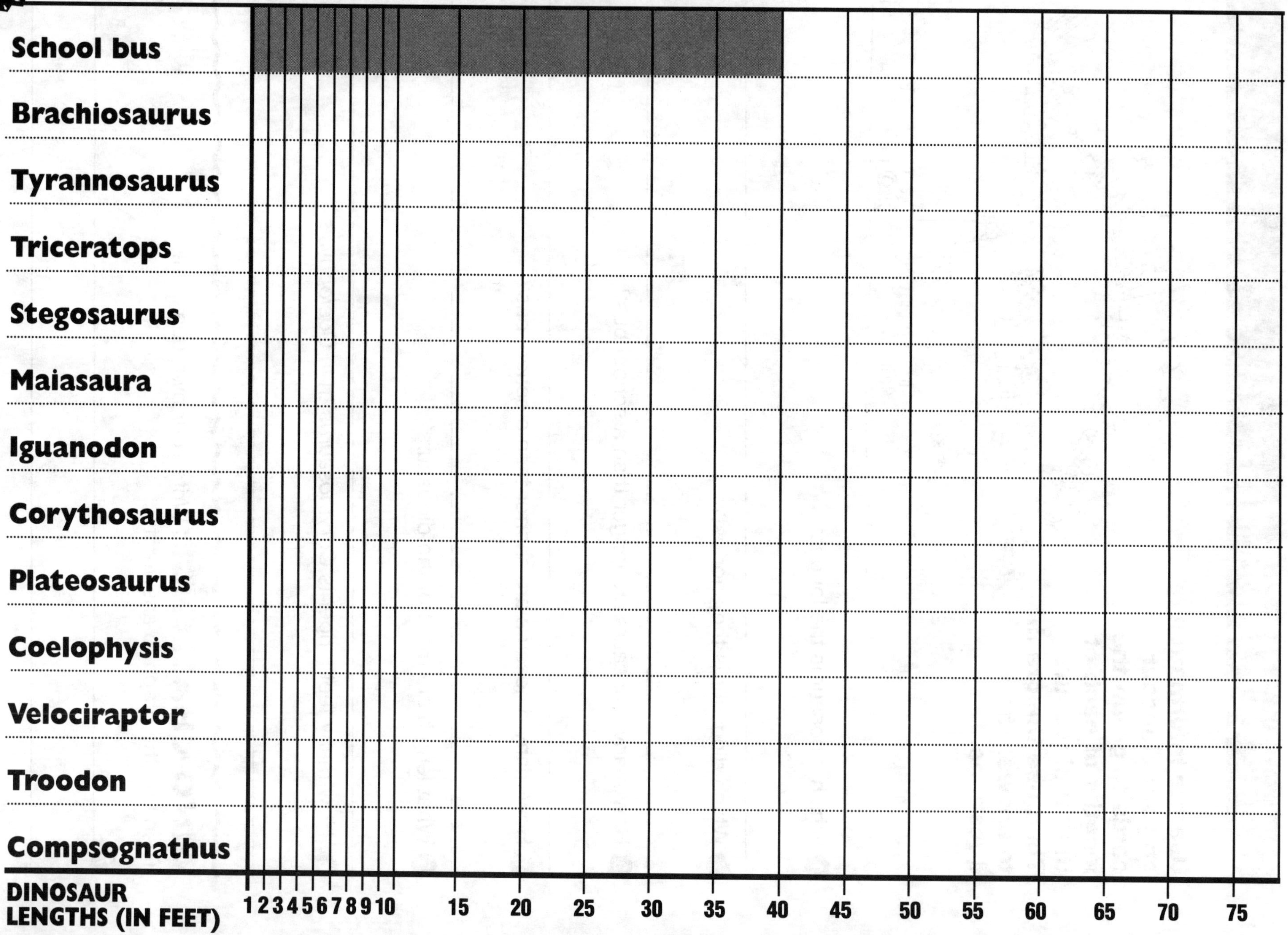
School bus
Brachiosaurus
Tyrannosaurus
Triceratops
Stegosaurus
Maiasaura
Iguanodon
Corythosaurus
Plateosaurus
Coelophysis
Velociraptor
Troodon
Compsognathus
DINOSAUR LENGTHS (IN FEET)
1 2 3 4 5 6 7 8 9 10 15 20 25 30 35 40 45 50 55 60 65 70 75

Life-Size Velociraptor Puzzle

8 1/2 INCHES

11 INCHES

5 1/2 FEET

3 1/2 FEET

VELOCIRAPTOR

25 26 27 28 29 30
19 20 21 22 23 24
13 14 15 16 17 18
7 8 9 10 11 12
1 2 3 4 5 6

Dinosaur Wheel of Fame

Cut out both wheels along the dashed lines, including the window on Wheel A. Put wheel A on top of wheel B. Poke a brass fastener through the dot to attach them. Then turn the wheel to learn some exciting dinosaur facts!

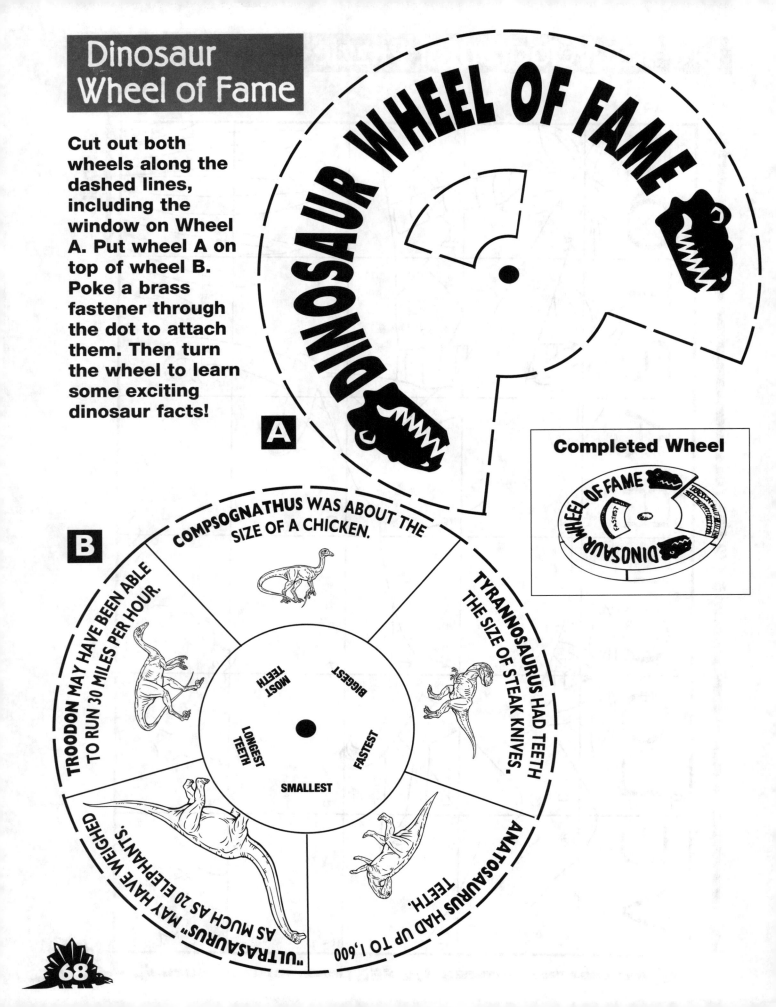

A

DINOSAUR WHEEL OF FAME

Completed Wheel

B

COMPSOGNATHUS WAS ABOUT THE SIZE OF A CHICKEN.

TROODON MAY HAVE BEEN ABLE TO RUN 30 MILES PER HOUR.

TYRANNOSAURUS HAD TEETH THE SIZE OF STEAK KNIVES.

MOST TEETH

BIGGEST

LONGEST TEETH

FASTEST

SMALLEST

"ULTRASAURUS" MAY HAVE WEIGHED AS MUCH AS 20 ELEPHANTS.

ANATOSAURUS HAD UP TO 1,600 TEETH.

68

UNDERSTANDING PALEONTOLOGY

What are fossils?
What can we learn from them?

Fossils are the organic remains of prehistoric plants or animals; they are also the records of ancient life on Earth. Whether taking the form of bones, teeth, or eggs, fossils provide scientists with tangible links to the past. Together, these remains show changes in plant and animal life over time and provide information about shifts in climate and even geography. Fossils can also be compared to the living things of today, providing clues to present-day adaptation and behavior. For example, dinosaur bones share many communalities with contemporary birds, leading paleontologists to believe that these long-extinct creatures were the ancestors of our feathered friends.

How are dinosaurs preserved?

Dinosaur fossils are often found in layers of sedimentary rocks such as sandstone and mudstone. How do these remains, laid down in ancient rock, find their way to the Earth's surface? Here's one story.

1 The dinosaur dies. It sinks to the bottom of an ancient river or lake, or is buried in a sand dune.

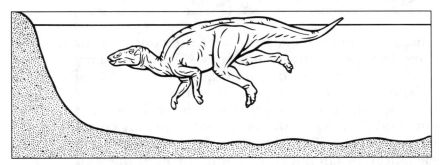

2 The dinosaur's body rots or is eaten by scavengers, until only its skeleton, or a few bones, remains.

Deinonychus *claw*

Maiasaura *eggshell*

Maiasaura *vertebrae*

Hadrosaur jaw

69

3 Layers of sediment build up over the bones. Minerals collect in the small spaces of the bones, making them harder and heavier. This process turns them into fossils.

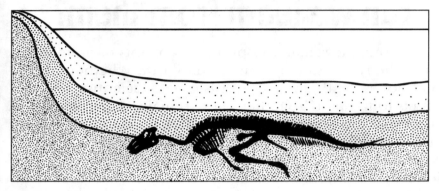

4 The water dries up. Over millions of years, the rock erodes and the fossils are exposed.

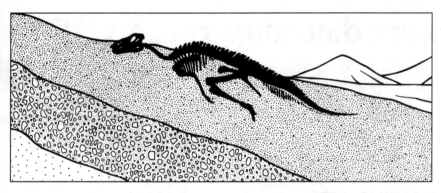

This chain of events—occurring over the course of many million years—happens only in lucky cases. Why? So many elements can conspire to destroy dinosaur bones and fossils. For example, if the animal died on land, scavengers might have fed on its dead body, leaving the exposed bones to crack and dry up in the hot sun. And even when the bones were quickly covered by sediments, they could still be destroyed by mountain-building activity, glaciation, or chemicals leaching through the soil.

What are trace fossils? What can we learn from them?

Unlike a regular fossil, which is the actual remains of a prehistoric animal or plant, a trace fossil provides indirect evidence of an organism's existence. Tracks, burrows, and skin imprints are all trace fossils. How were they formed? First, an ancient organism left its impression on sand or mud before rotting away. Then, over millions of years, that impression hardened into rock, or a trace

Dinosaur coprolite

Dinosaur footprint

Dino Chuckle!

Q. What do you call fossils that are laying down?

A. Lazybones!

Ancient fossilized plants

fossil. *Coprolites*, the scientific term for the fossil remains of animal dung, are trace fossils, too. Are these types of remains as important to researchers as regular fossils? Absolutely. Trace fossils provide many valuable clues about the lives of the mighty dinosaurs. For example, tracks help paleontologists to determine:

▶ whether dinosaurs walked on two or four legs (absense of front footprints indicate that some species moved on two legs);

▶ whether dinosaurs traveled in herds (numerous and overlapping prints of the same species is a sign of herding);

▶ whether dinosaurs fought with one another (two sets of prints in a chaotic pattern can indicate a struggle);

▶ whether dinosaurs dragged their tails (the lack of tail impressions probably means that most dinosaurs held their tails erect);

▶ how fast dinosaurs moved (distance between consistent prints is a sign of speed);

▶ and of course, how big dinosaurs' feet were.

Likewise, there is much to learn from skin impressions. These imprints, which are rare, provided the first strong evidence that dinosaurs' skin was scaly. Coprolites are telling, too. Paleontologist Karen Chin has distinguished herself in this important area of dinosaur science. By studying fossilized droppings, she has learned a great deal about the diets of these enormous creatures.

That's a Fact!

The largest dinosaur skull ever found was 10 feet wide and 8 feet high. It belonged to a Ceratopsian dinosaur.

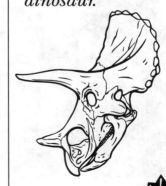

Where have dinosaur bones been found?

PERIOD KEY
Triassic ▲
(245-208 years ago)
Jurassic ●
(208-135 years ago)
Cretaceous ■
(135-65 years ago)

The remains of dinosaurs have been found all over the world and on every continent—from North America to Asia to frozen Antarctica. Why? Because all the continents were connected during the beginning of the Triassic Period. And even as they drifted apart, some land bridges remained, enabling dinosaurs to simply walk from one continent to another. As a result, the fossils of certain related species have been unearthed all over the planet. Armored dinosaurs, for example, are found in the United Kingdom, North and South America, Antarctica, and Australia. But this is not true of all species. By the Cretaceous Period, many dinosaurs—isolated by seas—diversified and adapted to the particular conditions of their habitats. For example, giant horned dinosaurs, like *Triceratops*, have only been found in western North America.

Montana badlands

How do paleontologists decide where to dig?

Paleontologists often use geologic maps and satellite photographs to help them decide the best spots for digging up dinosaur bones. They look for areas where there are sedimentary rock layers, which are known to be between 245 to 65 million years old—the time of the dinosaurs. Sometimes they locate sites where fossils have already been found because it's a good bet that more will be there.

Large outcrops of eroding sedimentary rock, called *badlands*, are frequently good places to find dinosaur bones. These barren, constantly eroding rock exposures hold no topsoil and few plants, which means paleontologists can see—and get to—fossils more easily. But even in badlands, fossil finds are pretty rare. Often, paleontologists and site crews will spend weeks searching for remains, but find only rocks and the occasional rusty can. Good luck plays an important role. Sometimes fossils are found in places where paleontologists would least expect to locate them. For example, in 1878, a group of workers in a Belgian coal mine accidentally made one of the best discoveries ever—skeletons of nearly 40 *Iguanodons!*

What happens at a fossil site? What tools are used?

When paleontologists get to an area that they think might contain dinosaur remains, the first thing they do is visually survey the site. They look carefully for specific sediments that might contain fossils and places where fossils might be weathering out of the ground. Usually, paleontologists get down on their hands and knees to better inspect the sediments and fossils. If the site looks promising, the paleontologist and crew may dig a small trench to find the fossil-bearing rock layer. Once it is located, and more fossils are uncovered, a full excavation begins.

Let's pretend you're a paleontologist who has just discovered a dinosaur bone. The first thing you'll want to do is record where you found it in your field notebook. You'll need to make some notes regarding how it is positioned in the ground and map out the site. To do this, you'll set up a square meter grid around the bone to mark its location. Next, you'll carefully remove some of the dirt and loose rock that's surrounding the bone. A tool called an *awl* can help you accomplish this task. A whisk broom is then used to wipe away any loose pieces of rock near the bone. If the rock around the bone is very hard, you may need to use a chisel to remove it. As the bone is gradually exposed, a special kind of glue may be applied to help stabilize it, or keep it from crumbling.

Once the dirt and excess rock is removed from around the bone, you'll make notes in your field book regarding its apparent shape and size. How is it positioned in the ground? Is it part of a skeleton or is it isolated? Does it show signs of weathering? scavenging?

Jack Horner applies special glue

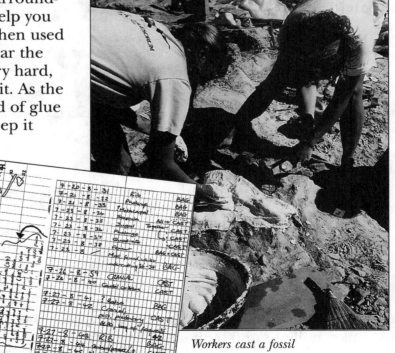

Workers cast a fossil

Page from a field notebook

After you've documented the bone in the ground, you are ready to remove it. To do this, you'll need to make a plaster jacket for it. A plaster cast, similar to the kind doctors put on broken arms, will help protect it on its journey back to the museum. Jacketing a bone requires several steps. First you'll need to cover the exposed portion of the bone with damp paper towels. Next, you'll cover that with burlap strips that have been dipped in plaster. After the plaster has dried, it's time to cut away the rock supporting the bottom side of the bone, tip it over, and repeat the plastering process on the bottom half. When the bone is completely protected, it is ready to be shipped back to the museum's preparation lab.

Tools of the Trade

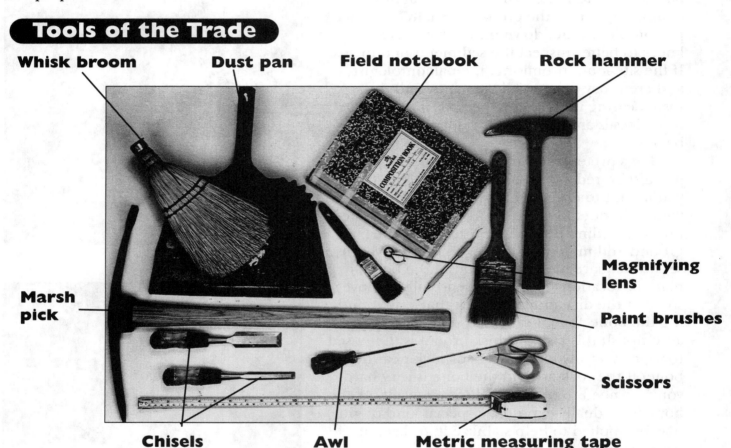

Whisk broom

Dust pan

Field notebook

Rock hammer

Magnifying lens

Paint brushes

Scissors

Marsh pick

Chisels

Awl

Metric measuring tape

What do paleontologists find at a fossil site?

It is very exciting to unearth a complete or partial dinosaur skeleton, but such finds are extremely rare. Paleontologists keep very busy though. They are always on the lookout for remains that will tell them more about life in the past. At dig sites, paleontologists find many incredible things including bones, bone fragments, eggs, dung, teeth, footprints, worm holes, and root casts from trees. All of these serve as clues and help to tell the story of the dinosaurs—how they behaved, what they ate, and what their environments were like, millions and millions of years ago.

Hadrosaur bone bed

Orodromeus *nest*

Do "regular people" ever find dinosaur bones?

You bet! Amateur fossil hunters have made key contributions to the study of dinosaurs by acting responsibly and sharing their finds with experts in the field. For example, in 1988, Kathy Wankel and her family were on a fishing trip in eastern Montana when they stumbled upon an odd-looking bone sticking out of the ground. Kathy brought a few fragments of the bone to the Museum of the Rockies. Then a few of the museum staff went out to the site where she found them to take a look. The bone, as it turned out, belonged to one of the most complete *Tyrannosaurus rex* skeletons every found. And in honor of Kathy, that famous dinosaur skeleton is now known as the Wankel T. rex.

Amateur fossil hunters like Kathy are encouraged to work with professional paleontologists when uncovering fossils of any kind. Why? Much of the information that is needed to expand our understanding of life in the past *has* to be collected when fossils are still in the ground.

That's a Fact!

It's against the law to remove fossils from private or government property without permission.

A young field worker helps dig up a dinosaur

75

ACTIVITIES

Dinosaurs Lived Here: Dig-Site Map (Geography)

Dinosaur bones have been found all over the world and on every continent! To familiarize students with the major international dig sites and to sharpen their map-reading skills, make photocopies of pages 85 and 86. Distribute a set to each child (or cooperative group). Encourage children to explore the map, familiarizing themselves with the seven continents, the Period Key, and the Compass Rose. Then invite them to use the map to answer the questions on page two of the reproducible. Follow up the activity with questions such as: Why do you think there is only one dig site in Antarctica? How do you think dinosaurs got from one continent to another?

To Extend Learning
Supplement "Dinosaurs Lived Here" with a short lesson on continental drift (for information on this topic, see page 13).

Geology Sandwiches: A Hands-on Story About Rock Layers (Science)

Is a field trip to the badlands of Montana out of the question? Not to worry...constructing a Geology Sandwich is a wonderful way to introduce children to the important concept of rock layers. This hands-on activity will also help them to understand how geologists and paleontologists use clues in the rock to locate promising sites for digging up dinosaur fossils (for more information on these topics, see page 72).

What follows is a thumbnail script for you to read as the children assemble their sandwiches. It is intended as a model. Feel free to enrich it with personal insights and touches—you're the storyteller!

MATERIALS
▶ white bread   ▶ wheat bread   ▶ jelly
▶ plastic knives   ▶ peanut butter   ▶ bananas (cut into thin slices)

DIRECTIONS

1 Divide the class into pairs, providing each with plastic knives, white and wheat bread, and plastic containers filled with jelly, peanut butter, and banana slices.

2 Share with kids that the Earth's crust—or the ground on which we stand—is made up of stacks of different kinds of rock called *layers*. **Script:** *The good news is that some of the layers contain dinosaur fossils! The bad news is that those fossil-rich layers, which are millions of years old, are often buried beneath a number of newer layers of very hard rock (not to mention soil, grass, and plants).* To help students understand this concept, you might try a piggy bank analogy: *The coins dropped in a piggy bank a year ago will end up on the bottom, while those dropped in last week will be closer to the top.*

76

③ Have each pair take a slice of wheat bread. **Script:** *We're going to make Geology Sandwiches. Let's pretend this wheat bread is the oldest layer of rock in our sandwich. Let's say it's 200 million years old.*

④ Invite kids to spread a generous amount of peanut butter on the bread. **Script:** *Let's pretend this peanut butter is the second oldest layer of rock. Let's say it's 70 million years old. Were dinosaurs around 70 million years ago? (yes) Well it just so happens that when some of those dinosaurs died, their bones sunk into mud. Over thousands of years, the mud hardened into rock and the bones hardened into fossils.* Invite kids to press a few (four or five) banana slices into the peanut butter. **Script:** *Let's pretend these banana slices are the dinosaur fossils.*

⑤ Have kids spread a generous amount of jelly on top of the peanut butter. **Script:** *Another layer of rock formed on top of the peanut butter layer. Is it newer or older? (newer) Let's say it was formed 50 million years ago. Were there dinosaurs 50 million years ago? (no) Then paleontologists won't find any dinosaur bones in this layer.*

⑥ Have kids complete their geology sandwiches by placing a slice of white bread on top. **Script:** *Another rock layer formed on top of the jelly layer. Is it newer or older? (newer) Let's say it's 30 million years old. Pretend you are standing on top of the sandwich. Could you tell if there were fossils underneath? (no) This is the same problem that paleontologists face. That's why they look for places where a fossil is exposed or "peeking out." Many things can cause a fossil to be exposed, such as erosion. Erosion is when the top layers of rock are worn away by wind and rain. Would you see fossils if the white bread and jelly layer had eroded? (yes)*

⑦ **Script:** *Another thing that can expose fossil layers is an earthquake because it causes parts of the Earth to break apart. Let's say there was an earthquake.* Invite kids to cut their sandwiches in half. **Script:** *Do each of the sandwich layers look different? (yes) Real rock layers look different, too, because they are formed at different times out of different kinds of sand and mud. Do you see any fossils? (yes) Pretend you're a paleontologist: remove one.*

⑧ **Script:** *Which layer would you look in to find more dinosaur fossils? (peanut butter) This is how paleontologists work. When they see a certain kind of rock from a certain period (like the peanut butter), it tells them that other dinosaur fossils may be buried there, too.*

⑨ If possible, follow up the activity by sharing pictures or slides of the Grand Canyon, the Badlands, and/or other rock formations where layering is apparent. Finally, invite kids to eat their geology sandwiches. Bon appetit!

Mineralization Investigation (Science)

How do the bones of dinosaurs sometimes survive for millions and millions of years? Layers of sediment cover them up. Then, over time, minerals collect in the small spaces of the bones, making them harder and heavier—and turning them into fossils. To simulate the mineralization process, try this easy science experiment.

MATERIALS

- ▶ moist sponge
- ▶ a funnel or a straw
- ▶ measuring cup
- ▶ sand
- ▶ water
- ▶ bowl
- ▶ 4 tablespoons of salt

DIRECTIONS

1. Use the scissors to cut the sponge into the shape of a bone.

2. Place the sand inside the bowl. Bury the sponge in the sand. Explain to students that the bone represents a dinosaur bone covered with sediment.

3. Dissolve the salt in one cup of warm water.

4. Press the funnel (or straw) through the sand and into the buried sponge. then slowly pour the salt water down through the funnel and into the sponge. When the sponge is full of liquid, stop pouring. (If need be, dig up the sponge and check to make sure it's saturated.) Explain to kids that salt water represents the mineral solution that fills in the empty spaces of dinosaur bones, causing them to fossilize. These minerals come from rain water, which seeped down into the ground and into the buried bones.

5. Set the experiment aside in a warm place.

6. After about a week, use your finger to gently dig down into the sand until you strike the bone. Check to see it has fully hardened. If it has, use a spoon or brush to continue digging. Work carefully until the bone is completely exposed. (You will probably find that part of the crystal mixture soaked into the sand, as well; that's okay.) Then carefully remove your fossilized dinosaur bone.

Invite students to examine the bone. Ask: How has it changed? What made it hard? (The sponge, like a bone, soaked up the salt, which is a mineral.) What happened to the water? (It evaporated.) Guide kids to understand that similar changes took place in real dinosaur bones, over the course of thousands of years and with different minerals.

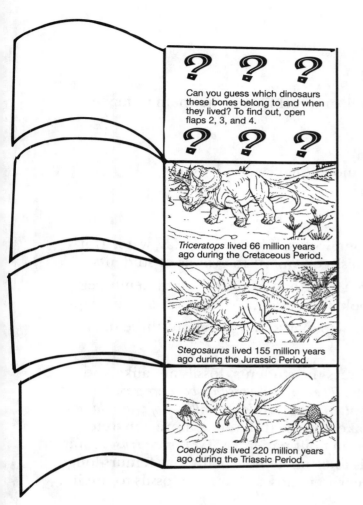

Can you guess which dinosaurs these bones belong to and when they lived? To find out, open flaps 2, 3, and 4.

Triceratops lived 66 million years ago during the Cretaceous Period.

Stegosaurus lived 155 million years ago during the Jurassic Period.

Coelophysis lived 220 million years ago during the Triassic Period.

Digging Down Deep Flapbook (Langauge Arts)

Paleontologists can tell how old dinosaur fossils are by figuring out the age of the rock the fossils are found in (see page 93 for more information). Reinforce this fact by inviting each student to assemble a Digging Down Deep Flapbook. Make double-sided photocopies of pages 87 and 88 (be careful not to invert the copy on the second sheet). Distribute a copy to each child, guiding him or her to cut along the solid (horizontal) lines, and fold along the dashed (vertical) line to make the flapbook (as show on the left). Students can then read and explore their flapbooks.

Follow up the activity by asking questions such as: What do these dinosaurs have in common with the rock they are buried in? (the dinosaur bones are from the same period). Why might rock from these periods become exposed? (erosion) Do you think it is easier for paleontologists to dig down deep or to look for exposed rock from these periods? Why?

Picture This!: Bone-Bed Map (Math, Science)

Before dinosaur fossils are removed from a dig site, paleontologists carefully draw a map that shows each bone's position in the ground. Why? These maps help them to learn more about how the dinosaurs lived and died. Make photocopies of the simulated bone-bed map on page 89 and distribute one to each child. Challenge kids to color each bone type its assigned color, then do a bone-type inventory. When everyone is finished, follow up the activity with questions such as: Why do you think paleontologists make maps of the bones when they are in the ground? (Possible Answers: This provides clues about how the animals died and ancient geography; it helps paleontologists keep track of what they've found.) Why do you think all of these dinosaur bones were found in one area? (Possible answers: The water washed them all to the same spot; the animals died at the same time; the animals lived together in a family or herd.) Why do you think more teeth were found than skulls? (Possible answer: Each dinosaur had many teeth, but only one skull.)

To Extend Learning
Invite children to represent their bone-type inventories as a bar graph.

Make a Fossil (Art, Science)

To help kids understand what dinosaur fossils look and feel like, invite them to make some fossils of their own.

MATERIALS
▶ reproducible page 90 ▶ self-drying modeling clay ▶ water
▶ newspapers (to cover tables) ▶ art smocks

DIRECTIONS

❶ Reproduce and distribute a Copycat Page, along with self-hardening clay, water (for wetting the clay), and newspapers (to cover desks or tables) to groups of students.

❷ Challenge students to choose a fossil type from the Copycat Page—tooth, femur, egg, digit, vertebrae—or one from a reference book, then craft a 3-D version of it in clay.

❸ When everyone's finished, set the fossils on newspaper to dry for about three days.

To Extend Learning

Follow up the activity, by brainstorming a list of ways the students' fossils are alike and different from real dinosaur fossils. (For example: *They are alike because both are grey, both are hard, and both are fragile. They are different because: real dinosaur fossils are millions of years old, are formed from bone, and are usually much bigger.*) To make the size difference more concrete, draw a life-size femur on the board or cut one from craft paper. (A *Tyrannosaurus* femur is about three to four feet long.) Challenge kids to estimate how many clay femurs-long the real femur is. Then use the clay femur to see who is closest. Save the fossils to use in one of the Simulated Digs, which follows.

Simulated Digs (Science)

Few activities are more fun—or more informative—than a simulated dinosaur dig.
To prepare, share information about real dinosaur digs with students. (There are many fine children's books on the topic; see the Resource List on page 111.) Decide whether you want your dig site to be outside or inside; instructions for both options follow. Then roll up your sleeves and dig in!

OUTDOOR DIG

MATERIALS
▶ reproducible page 91 ▶ student-made fossils
▶ stakes, string ▶ old paintbrushes and/or toothbrushes
▶ boxes, newspaper, masking tape ▶ camera and film
▶ plastic shovels, plastic dustpans

DIRECTIONS

1 A few days before the big event, send home a note requesting that students wear play clothes on dig day. They'll probably get pretty dirty!

2 Select and prepare a dig site—a large mound of dirt, an unplanted flower bed, or a playground sandbox are great spots. Bury 15 to 30 student-made fossils (see page 80).

3 Use stakes and string to mark the borders of the dig site.

4 Bring students to the site. Explain that at a real dig, people work as a cooperative team. Some of their jobs include: diggers, artists/recorders, cleaners/packers, and on-site photographers. Invite children to decide which position they wish to have, then model the responsibilities of each (see below). Encourage kids to choose jobs that match their special abilities.

5 Now it's time to get started. Invite the diggers to use shovels, brushes, and dustpans to carefully unearth fossils. After the fossils are removed from the ground, the artists/recorders should fill in the Dig This! Data Sheet by drawing each fossil, filling in the fossil type (if known), recording its length in centimeters, and jotting down any observations. Next, the cleaners/packers should brush any remaining dirt from the fossils, wrap them carefully in newspaper, and pack them in boxes to be shipped to the classroom laboratory. During this whole process, the on-site photographers should take photos of the fossils, as well as of their classmates at work.

6 When all the fossils have been unearthed, work together to choose a perfect name for your dig site. That name might reflect the location of the dig site —"Schoolosaurus"— or its spoils—"Femurland."

7 Take the fossils back to your classroom. If you like, display them on a Dig Site Discovery Table, encouraging kids to explore them on their own.

8 Follow up the activity by inviting children to reflect on their jobs and to share their thoughts and observations with the class. What did they like about the task? What didn't they like? Why is it important to cooperate? Invite the artists/recorders to share their data. What kind of fossils did they find the most of? the least of? What conclusions might paleontologist draw from the findings?

9 Display the photos on an "Our Day at the Dig" bulletin board, inviting students to write captions for each.

To Extend Learning
Publish a class-created *Dig Big Book*, complete with text and photos. Invite student volunteers to read the book to younger students or to parents during open house.

INDOOR DIG

MATERIALS
▶ reproducible page 91
▶ large, sturdy cardboard box (at least 3 by 4 feet)
▶ sand or dried corn cob (available at pet stores)
▶ plastic shovels, plastic dustpans
▶ old paintbrushes and/or toothbrushes
▶ newspaper
▶ craft knife, duct tape

DIRECTIONS
1 Using a craft knife, cut off the upper portion of a large cardboard box so that it stands about 10 inches high. Seal the bottom of the box with duct tape to minimize leakage.

2 Choose an out-of-the-way corner of your room to use as a dig site. Place the box on top of several sheets of newspaper. Next, fill the box with about five to seven inches of sand or kekob. Bury 10 to 30 student-made fossils (see page 90).

3 Divide the class into cooperative groups of three or four, which will take turns at the dig site.

4 Invite the first group to work at the site. Reproduce and distribute a Dig This! Data Sheet to each member. Make sure each child is equipped with the necessary tools: a plastic shovel, a paintbrush or toothbrush, a dustpan, and a centimeter ruler (assembled from the Dig This! Data Sheet).

5 Tell kids that they are going to participate in a simulated dinosaur dig. Stress that real paleontologists must be cooperative, patient, and, above all, extremely careful, to ensure that the fossils they uncover are not damaged. Model the correct way to dig: Use the shovel and dustpan to locate a fossil. After a fossil is discovered or "tapped," switch to a brush to unearth the entire fossil. Next, lift the fossil carefully out of the

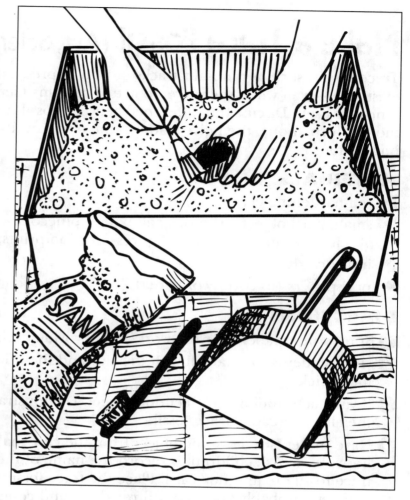

bone bed and place it on a sheet of newspaper. Then fill in the Dig This! Data Sheet by drawing and measuring the fossil, noting the fossil type (if known), and recording observations (if any).

6 After the group has unearthed all their fossils, encourage them to pool and discuss their data by posing questions such as: What bone type did you find the most of? The least of? What was the measurement of the longest bone you found? The shortest? Which bone types tended to be the biggest? and so on.

7 Finally, challenge the group to give their dig site a great name, just as real diggers do (for suggestions, see the "Outdoor Dig").

8 When the first group has finished its dig, re-bury the fossils and invite the next group to the bone bed. (You can choose to do all the digs in one day or one dig a day for a week.) After each group has had an opportunity to dig, bring the class together to discuss the experience.

To Extend Learning

If you like, cap off the activity by reading Aliki's *Digging Up Dinosaurs!* How was their classroom dig like a real dig? How was it different?

Make a Trace Fossil (Art, Science)

Trace fossils, such as dinosaur tracks or skin impressions, provide evidence of a dinosaur's existence—even when there are no actual remains (such as fossilized bones) of the dinosaur itself. Discuss the difference between fossils and trace fossils (see page 70 for more information), then give students the opportunity to create some of these telling impressions.

MATERIALS

▶ self-hardening clay

▶ small, hard objects (shells, small bones, pinecones, twigs, old keys, paper clips, coins, plastic dinosaurs and action figures—for footprints, etc.)

▶ index cards

▶ newspapers (to cover work area)

DIRECTIONS

1 Spread newspaper over the work area. Provide each child with a fist-sized lump of clay.

2 Have students form a ball with the clay and then flatten it until it is just less than an inch thick.

3 Invite each student to select one object. Demonstrate how to press the material into the clay to create a trace fossil.

4 Have students remove the object from the clay, making sure it has made an impression. Ask children to record the name of the object they used to create their trace fossil on an index card. Place the trace fossils in an out-of-the-way place to dry (this will probably take about three days) and collect the index cards.

5 After the trace fossils have dried, place them, along with the stack of index cards, on a Trace Fossil Discovery Table. Then challenge groups of students to match the objects named on the cards with the correct trace fossils. Can anyone get them all right?

To Extend Learning
Follow up the activity by asking questions such as: What objects were easiest to identify? The hardest? Why? How might trace fossils help paleontologists learn about dinosaurs? If you like, make a class chart listing things that can and cannot be determined by examining trace fossils. Hang it on the wall for kids to revisit throughout your dinosaur unit.

Dinosaurs Lived Here: Dig-Site Map

Name _____

The ▲, ●, and ■ shapes mark places where dinosaur fossils have been found. The Period Key tells whether the fossils are from the Triassic, Jurassic, or Cretaceous period.

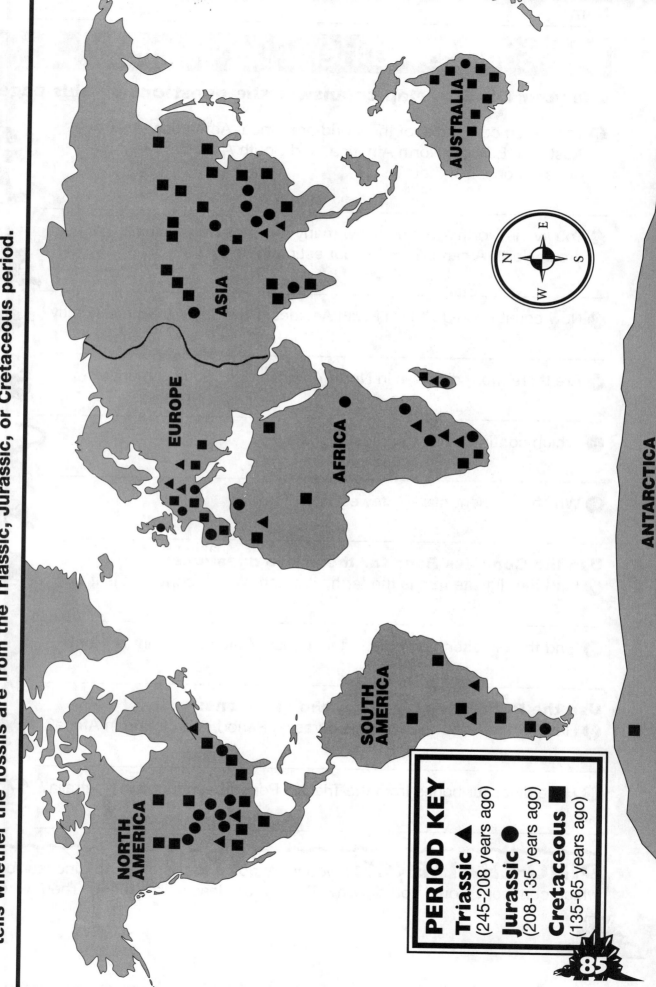

NORTH AMERICA

SOUTH AMERICA

EUROPE

ASIA

AFRICA

AUSTRALIA

ANTARCTICA

PERIOD KEY
Triassic ▲ (245–208 years ago)
Jurassic ● (208–135 years ago)
Cretaceous ■ (135–65 years ago)

Name _____

Use your Dig Site Map to answer the questions on this page.

1 The seven continents of the world are Africa, Antarctica, Asia, Australia, Europe, North America, and South America. Are there dig sites on all of them?

_____

2 You live in North America. How many dig sites do you think there are in North America? Write your estimate here.

_____

3 Now count the dig sites in North America. How many are there exactly?

_____

4 Are there more dig sites in North America or in South America?

_____

5 Which continent has the most dig sites?

_____

6 Which continent has the fewest dig sites?

_____

Use the Compass Rose for these two questions:
7 Find the dig site that is the farthest south. Which continent is it on?

_____

8 Find the dig site that is the farthest east. Which continent is it on?

_____

Use the Period Key for these two questions:
9 Have dinosaur bones from the Jurassic Period been found in Africa?

_____

10 Have dinosaur bones from the Triassic Period been found in Australia?

_____

DINO-CHALLENGE: If you were going to try to dig up dinosaur bones, which continent would you dig on? Share your ideas with a friend. Then write about it.

Digging Down Deep

These paleontologists are working on top of several layers of rock. If they dig down deep enough they will discover the bones of three different dinosaurs. Open flap 1.

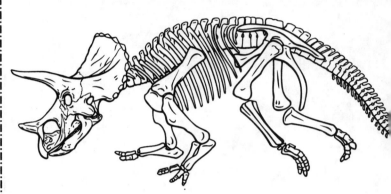

This rock was formed during the Cretaceous Period.

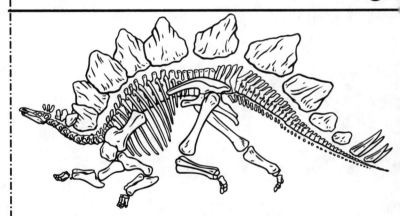

This rock was formed during the Jurassic Period.

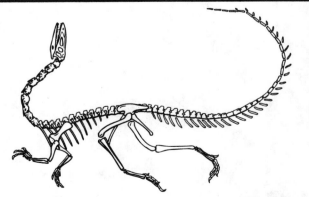

This rock was formed during the Triassic Period.

Can you guess which dinosaurs these bones belong to and when they lived? To find out, open flaps 2, 3, and 4.

Triceratops lived 66 million years ago during the Cretaceous Period.

Stegosaurus lived 155 million years ago during the Jurassic Period.

Coelophysis lived 220 million years ago during the Triassic Period.

Picture This!: Dig Site Map

Below is a drawing of a pretend dig site. It looks much like the ones that real paleontologists make. This site contained the bones of several *Maiasaura*. Use the Bone Key to color each of the five types of bones. Then count the bones and fill in the chart below. When you're finished, answer the questions.

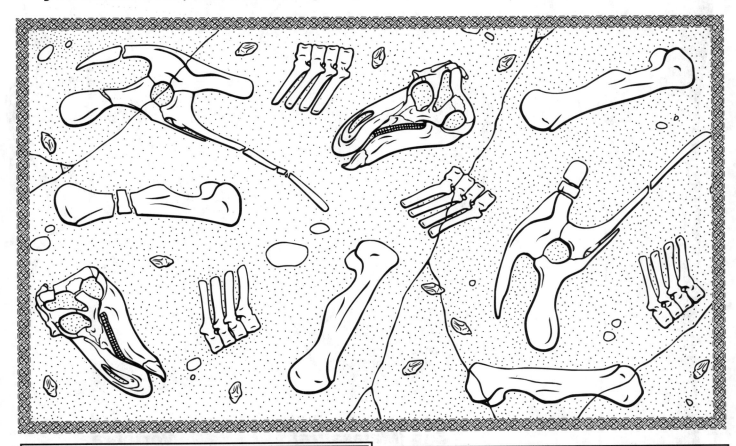

Bone Key

- ⬭ = tooth. Color each red.
- ⬭ = thigh bone. Color each blue.
- ⬭ = vertebrae. Color each green.
- ⬭ = hip bone. Color each yellow.
- ⬭ = skull. Color each purple.

Bone Type	Number Found
tooth	
thigh bone	
vertebrae	
hip bone	
skull	

❶ Which bone type did you find the most of? _____

❷ Which bone types did you find the least of? _____

89

Fossil Copycat Page

Look at the dinosaur fossils below. Then make one (or more) out of clay.

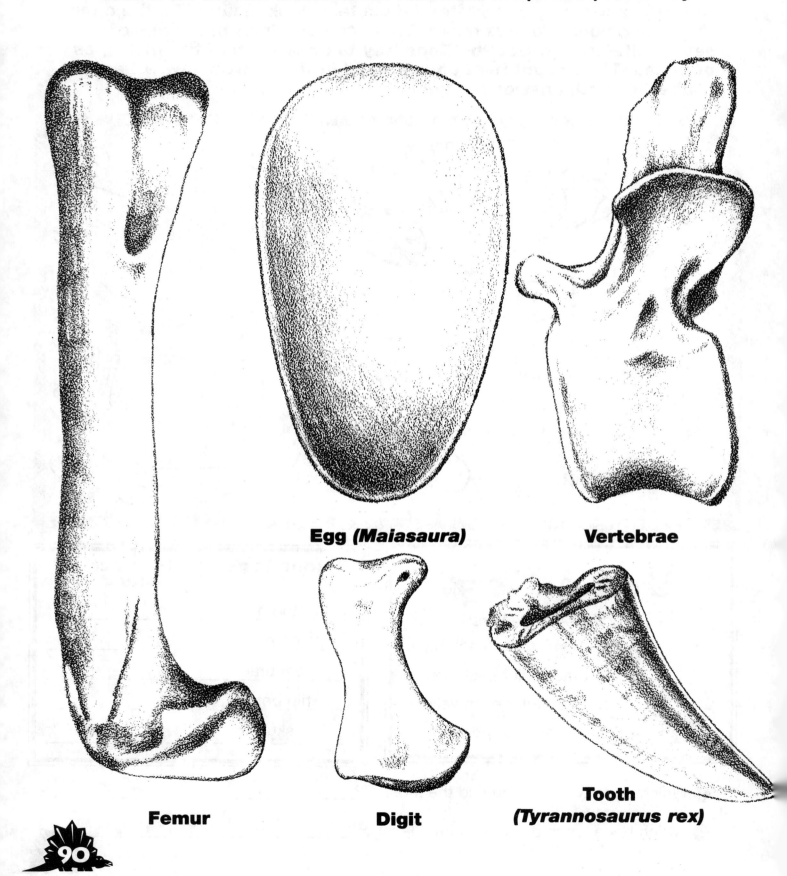

Egg (Maiasaura)

Vertebrae

Femur

Digit

**Tooth
(Tyrannosaurus rex)**

Dig This Data Sheet

Name(s): _____ Date: _____

Dig Site Name: _____

Use this data sheet to record each fossil you find at your dig site. We filled in the first one for you. To measure the fossils, use the centimeter ruler on the right. (To make it, cut out the two strips and tape or paste them together.) When you're finished, give your dig site a great name.

Drawing of Fossil	Fossil Type	Length	Observations
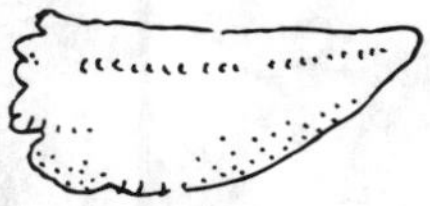	tooth	6 cm	Might be a T. rex tooth

26 27 28 29 30 31 32 33 34 35 36 37 38 39 40 41 42 43 44 45 46 47 48 49 50

1 2 3 4 5 6 7 8 9 10 11 12 13 14 15 16 17 18 19 20 21 22 23 24 25

Paste Here

THE SCIENCE OF STUDYING DINOSAURS FOSSILS

What happens to dinosaur bones when they arrive at a museum?

That's a Fact!

Some scientists estimate that less than one percent of all the dinosaurs species that ever lived have been discovered and described so far.

Broken and glued bone

At the end of a field season, paleontologists and crew members bring finds back to the Museum of the Rockies. At our labs, there is still a lot of work to be done. As soon as the dinosaur fossils arrive, our museum registrar makes a note of when they came in and what they are thought to be. Then our paleontologist and chief preparator (who heads the museum's lab) decide which ones should be cleaned first. For example, if a fossil specimen is going to be used in a research project or an exhibit, it gets top priority.

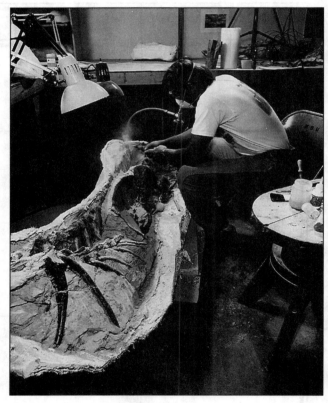

Preparator at work on an Allosaurus

The cleaning process is known as *fossil preparation.* Lab technicians, called *preparators,* clean the fossils so that they can be studied in greater detail. First, the preparators remove part of the plaster jacket so the rock around the bone is exposed. Then they begin to carefully clean away the excess dirt and rock, until only the fossil remains. Sometimes they have to dip the specimen in a weak acid bath to help remove the rock; other times, they use an air scribe to blast off the hardened dirt.

Once each fossil is cleaned, it is numbered, catalogued, and identified. If the bone is the first of its kind—which is pretty exciting—a paleontologist or graduate student will write a detailed description of it. The description is then printed in a professional journal such as the *Journal of Vertebrate Paleontology.* That way, new information can be shared with dinosaur enthusiasts all over the world.

How do paleontologists figure out what kinds of fossils they've found?

As paleontologists and preparators examine each fossil, they ask themselves key questions, such as: From what part of the body does this bone come? Is there anything that makes it distinct? Then the fossils are compared to the same bone types of other known species. Are there similarities in size, shape, and thickness? By mapping the presence and absence of these features, paleontologists can determine whether they've found the remains of a previously described or a brand-new species. They can also begin to trace the evolution of dinosaur groups. For example, evidence shows that Tyrannosaurids—such as *Albertosaurus*, *Daspletosaurus*, and *Tyrannosaurus rex*—each had powerful hind legs, a large skull, sharp teeth, stereoscopic vision, and two-fingered hands—which indicates that they were closely related on one another.

Preparator at work on a T. rex

How do paleontologists tell how old a bone is?

Paleontologists cannot date dinosaur bones, but they *can* date the rock around them. To do this, they rely on *radiometric*

Theropod tooth

dating, a process that detects the amount of radioactive decay that has occurred since the rocks were formed, and compares it to known rates of decay. Radiometric dating works best in volcanic ash deposits.

A second type of dating, which is more commonly used, is called *relative dating*. In this case, paleontologists make notes about the kinds of fossils they are finding in a certain rock layer and compare them to fossils that they know come from older rock layers and younger rock layers. This method helps them determine the approximate age of the fossils in question.

Can paleontologists tell the difference between male and female dinosaurs?

Paleontologists cannot definitively tell the difference between "boy" and "girl" dinosaurs. They are working on it, though. For example, they *can* see evidence of *dimorphism*, or differences in skeletal size and shape. By studying several skeletons of the same species, paleontologists have noted that some bones and, consequently, skeletons are bigger and more robust than others. What has this got to do with gender? It has been hypothesized that female dinosaurs had the larger skeletons. The theory holds that females would have needed the extra bone mass to support the formation of eggs. The calcium necessary to form eggs would have come from a mother dinosaur's bones.

Other clues to dinosaur gender may lie in their ornamentation. The species *Protoceratops*, for example, shows variation in crest size, which may indicate a differentiation in sex. Those with bigger crests are thought to be males. Paleontologists think they probably used these fancy head ornaments to attract the attention of females.

Can paleontologists ever tell if a dinosaur was sick or injured?

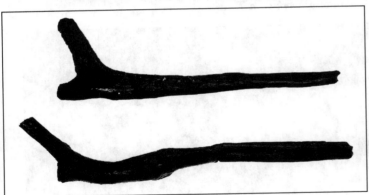

Bottom rib bone shows break and healing

Yes. Fossils tell paleontologists that dinosaurs were susceptible to bone breaks and damage—injuries that may have been caused by accidents, stress, predator attacks, or competition among members of the same species. In some cases, a fossil shows a break that has healed completely (often evidenced by excess bone growth around an injury). But in other cases, a fossil shows that healing was incomplete, which could mean that infection or loss of limb was that dinosaur's prime cause of death.

Paleontologists sometimes examine fossils with an eye toward pinpointing the most common injuries of a certain species. Darren Tanke of the Royal Tyrrell Museum of Paleontology found many broken and rehealed ribs and broken tail vertebrae among the hadrosaurs in the museum's collection. This leads him to believe that male hadrosaur may have fought one another—and kicked each other in the ribs. Tanke also theorizes that broken tail vertebrae may have been caused by hadrosaurs accidentally stepping on the tails of resting herd members. These studies do not substantiate hadrosaur behavior, but they *do* provide some new and intriguing pieces to the puzzle of their lifestyle.

Fossils also provide clues to dinosaurs' ailments. For example, a number of abnormally shaped or fused bones have been found, suggesting that these animals had their share of bone diseases and/or birth defects. Unfortunately, it is usually difficult to diagnose specific types of disease from fossil evidence.

How do dinosaurs get their names?

What do Chinese paleontologists call *Stegosaurus* and *Triceratops*? *Stegosaurus* and *Triceratops!* In fact, paleontologists the world over speak the same language when it comes to dinosaur names. Why? Common labels make it easier for them to share information with fellow scientists in Russia, France, the United States, Ghana—and every country in between.

Dinosaur names are usually formed from Greek or Latin roots. They generally

Dinosaur Names Defined

Barapasaurus: bird + legged + lizard

Compsognathus: elegant + jaw

Dryosaurus: oak + lizard

Gallimimus: rooster + mimic

Hypacrosaurus: very + high + ridged + lizard

Lycorhinus: wolf + snout

Mussaurus: mouse + lizard

Opisthocoelicaudia: backwards + hollow + tail

Titanosaurus: Titanic + lizard

Vulcanodon: fire + tooth

Hypacrosaurus *model*

have two parts—a first name and a last name. The first name (the *genus*) often describes a distinct characteristic of the animal, while the second name (the *species*) usually identifies an important person or a place that is linked to the discovery of the animal. For example, *Maiasaura peeblesorum* means: "good mother lizard from the Peebles Ranch." Jack Horner, who discovered this species, had the honor of picking its name. He chose *good mother* because there was a lot of evidence that this dinosaur was an active parent; he chose *peeblesorum* because he studied its remains on the Montana ranch of a family named Peebles.

That's a Fact!

The paleontologist named Alan Grant in Jurassic Park *was loosely based on the real Jack Horner.*

The Future According to Jack Horner

"Can we clone a dinosaur? Maybe someday; but remember, we can't even clone a worm yet."

"In the future, everyone will know more about dinosaurs than I do."

What is the future of paleontology?

State-of-the-art technologies are changing the way paleontologists study bones. For example:

► CAT scan machines enable scientists to look at the interiors of eggs, bones, and skulls. Some of the things they can see using CAT scans include: baby bones in fossilized eggs, growth rings in bones, and the braincase or nasal passages in skulls.

► Research on bone tissues offer new insight into bone growth that can be compared with other living animals.

► High-powered microscopes can identify genetic markers, such as DNA, further determining dinosaurs' relationships to each other and to different animals.

Dinosaur egg showing embrionic bone

With each new technology and fossil, scientists are better able to piece together the mysterious picture of life in the past. And as paleontologists gain access into unexplored areas in South American, Africa, and Central Asia, they will no doubt make important finds that will bring the lives of the dinosaurs into even sharper focus. Who knows what exciting facts the children of today's children will be reciting about *Maiasaura*, or *Brachiosaurus*, or *Tyrannosaurus rex*. But one thing is clear—kids and adults alike will always be fascinated by these incredible creatures.

ACTIVITIES

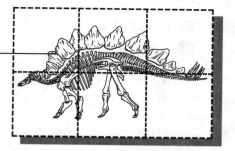

Dino-Magic Puzzle (Math, Science)

Dinosaur skeletons don't come fully assembled! Rather, paleontologists rely on educated guesses to figure out how the bones fit together. To illustrate their difficult task, distribute double-sided photocopies of pages 101–102 to each child (being careful not to invert the image on the back side). Challenge students to assemble their dinosaur puzzles, guess which dinosaur the skeleton belongs to, then turn over the pieces one by one to see what the dinosaur looked like when it was alive. Follow up the activity by asking questions such as: Was it difficult to put your dinosaur skeleton together? Why do you think it is even tougher for paleontologists to do this job? Would you like to have the job of making dinosaur models? Why or why not?

To Extend Learning

Provide kids with pictures of complete dinosaur skeletons (enlarged and photocopied from dinosaur reference books). Invite students to make their own puzzles by cutting the pictures into five to ten pieces. They can then try to reassemble them and/or trade them with classmates.

What Tracks Tell Us (Reflective Thinking)

Fossilized dinosaur tracks (called *trace fossils*) speak volumes about the giants that created them millions of years ago. Share information about what paleontologists can learn from these important fossil records (see page 70). Then distribute a photocopy of page 103 to each student, inviting them to study the footprints and make educated guesses about what happened when the tracks were first laid down. Follow up the activity by inviting students to share and compare their track stories.

To Extend Learning

Big dinosaurs took big steps! Help kids visualize this fact with some fun estimation activities. Take kids to an open area such as the gym or the playground. Have students measure the stride length of a *Tyrannosaurus rex:* 12 feet. Tape (or stake) that distance on the floor (or ground). Then invite kids to guess:

▶ How many of your steps will fit in a *T. rex* stride?

▶ How many strides would it take a *T. rex* to cross the room or parking lot?

After kids have recorded their estimates, encourage cooperative groups to find out the answers, then share their data with classmates. What might account for different answers to the same question?

Potato Footprint Stories (Art)

Tap kids' creativity by inviting them to create Potato Footprint Stories about the lives of their favorite dinosaurs.

MATERIALS

▶ potatoes
▶ craft knife
▶ paint smocks

▶ tempura paint
▶ old margarine tubs
▶ butcher paper

▶ ballpoint pen
▶ newspaper

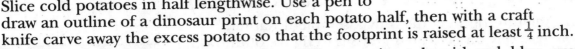

Plant-eater   Meat-eater   Baby

DIRECTIONS

❶ Prepare three or more potato footprint stamps. At the very least, you'll want to include a plant-eater, a meat-eater, and a baby (see templates at right). Slice cold potatoes in half lengthwise. Use a pen to draw an outline of a dinosaur print on each potato half, then with a craft knife carve away the excess potato so that the footprint is raised at least $\frac{1}{4}$ inch.

❷ Cover a large worktable with newspaper. Fill margarine tubs with red, blue, green, and yellow paint. Place the tubs, along with the footprint stamps and a big piece of craft paper for each student, on the table.

❸ Review a few plausible—and creative—track scenarios that kids might illustrate, such as some dinosaurs went for a drink, two dinosaurs got in a fight, a herd of dinosaurs passed through, and so on. Then invite students to use the footprint stamps to tell a dinosaur story.

To Extend Learning

Encourage students to write text to accompany their artwork. Share the visual and written stories with the class.

What Teeth Tell Us (Reflective Thinking)

Paleontologists have learned a lot about dinosaurs' eating habits by studying their fossilized teeth. The hands-on activity gives students the opportunity to do the same. Invite kids to cut out, sort, and paste the teeth beneath the dinosaurs they belong to. Reproduce and distribute page 104 to each child. (You may want to make sure kids have sorted correctly before they paste.) Then challenge children to use the teeth to conjecture about *Edmontosaurus*'s, *Diplodocus*'s, and *Tyrannosaurus*'s diets.

To Extend Learning

Follow up the activity by researching modern-day animals that are meat-eaters (dogs, cats, lions) and plant-eaters (cows, horses, elephants). What do their teeth tell us? How are their teeth like dinosaur teeth? Be sure to include people in your discussion. Are we plant- or meat-eaters? (Both. We have different kinds of teeth for different reasons: canine teeth for stabbing, incisors for biting, and molars for grinding.) How are our teeth like dinosaur teeth?

Doing Dinosaur Research (Science)

How do paleontologists figure out what kind of fossils they've uncovered at a dig site? Usually by comparing it to other fossils that have already been identified. This hands-on activity gives your students the opportunity to do research similar to that conducted by paleontologists and preparators in museums like the Museum of the Rockies. Photocopy page 105 and distribute one to each student. Invite children to compare the unidentified skull with the identified skulls, then use books to find out more about the mystery dinosaur: *Allosaurus.* (Be sure to have several dinosaur books on hands for kids to use; if you don't have a lot of resources, encourage kids to take turns doing their research.) After everyone has finished, challenge students to organize the information into a mini-report, or to write about the dinosaur in their journals.

To Extend Learning

Ask your local Fish, Wildlife and Parks Department to loan or donate some bones to your class. Then invite cooperative groups to sort the bones according to attributes—size, shape, color, texture, etc. Ask students to explain why they sorted them as they did. Do any of the bones look like they belong to the same animal? What makes students think so? If the animal species are known, challenge kids to guess which animals they belonged to, then share the correct answers with the class.

They're All Greek to Me: Naming Dinosaurs (Science)

Most dinosaur names are created by stringing two or more Greek (or Latin) root words together. *Maiasaura*, for example, links the word *Maia*, which means "good mother," to the word *saura*, which means "lizard." Research and discuss the names of some popular dinosaurs, asking kids why they think these species received the names they did. Then photocopy and distribute page 106 to each student. Challenge them to carefully examine the dinosaur pictures and choose a word from the Greek Dictionary to describe each one. Be sure to encourage kids to be creative, stressing that there are no wrong answers.

When everyone's finished, let students share their dinosaur names with classmates, explaining their choices. Finally, tell kids the species' real names (1: *Corythosaurus*; 2: *Styracosaurus*; 3: *Centiosaurus*; 4: *Psittocosaurus*; 5: *Struthiosaurus*). Did anybody choose the same ones? Why do you think paleontologists chose these names?

To Extend Learning

Follow up the activity by inviting students to create a name for an imaginary dinosaur by linking together four or more words from their Greek Dictionary such as *Allomegamyopoly-styrarhinosaurus* (weird-big-mouse-with-a-many-spiked-nose lizard). The longer—and sillier—the better! Then kids can draw their make-believe dinosaurs. Hang the drawings around the classroom to enjoy throughout your dinosaur unit.

Museum Dinosaurs Mini-Book (Language Arts)

What happens to dinosaur bones after they're removed from a dig site? Students can find out the answer to this question by constructing the mini-book entitled "Museum Dinosaurs." Make a double-sided photocopy of pages 107–108, and distribute a sheet to each student. Direct them as follows.

❶ Begin with the side that shows panels A, B, C, and D facing up.

❷ Cut the panels apart along the solid lines.

❸ Lay the panels on top of each other in alphabetical order, with the panel marked A on top.

❹ Staple the book along the dashed line. Complete the booklet by folding it along this line.

Then read the story with your class. Invite prereaders to use the pictures to retell the story and fluent readers to take turns reading the story to partners.

To Extend Learning
If possible, plan a trip to a museum in your area that displays models of dinosaurs (see list on page 111).

Culminating Activities (Cross-Curricular)

As your dinosaur unit draws to a close, invite cooperative groups or individual students to demonstrate what they've learned with a culminating activity. Here are a few ideas.

▶ **DINOSAUR BIG BOOK:** Kids can research, then publish a big book on their favorite dinosaur topic.

▶ **DINOSAUR POLL:** Challenge students to poll schoolmates on dinosaur-related topics, then graph or publish their findings. What conclusions can be drawn from this data?

▶ **DINOSAUR NEWSLETTER:** Publish a class-created "Dinosaur Times" newsletter. Each child—or group—is responsible for a different story. Don't forget to include a dinosaur puzzle and comic strip!

▶ **DINOSAUR DISCOVERY TABLE:** Encourage kids to contribute hands-on projects such as dioramas, puzzles, booklets, and audiotaped reports to a "Dinosaur Discovery Table." Then invite other classes to explore and learn.

▶ **DINOSAUR PLAY:** If dinosaurs could talk, what would they say? Have students write fanciful plays to perform for their classmates.

▶ **DINOSAUR PUPPET SHOW:** Children will have fun making dinosaur stick or finger puppets, then writing and performing the shows.

▶ **DINOSAUR LIFE TV SHOW:** Invite students to research, write, and present news stories, skits, and commentaries related to dinosaurs for a "Dinosaur Life" TV show. Videotape the show to share with parents and siblings.

▶ **DINOSAUR HABITAT BULLETIN BOARD:** Kids can research dinosaur habitats, then create a bulletin board display to share with classmates.

▶ **DINOSAUR DEBATES:** Children will enjoy researching, then orally presenting their views on hot topics such as, Which dinosaur was the greatest? How did the dinosaurs become extinct? Should independent fossil hunters be able to keep the fossils they find?

▶ **LIFE-SIZE DINOSAUR:** Work with your art teacher to build a huge papier-maché model of the kids' favorite species.

Jr. Paleontologist Certificates (Just for Fun)

Celebrate all you've learned about dinosaurs by presenting Jr. Paleontologist Certificates at an end-of-the-unit ceremony. Photocopy and distribute page 109 to each student. If you like, mark the occasion with a Dinosaur Shin-Dig— complete with dinosaur-shaped cookies, dinosaur read-alouds, and dinosaur dancing to the "Theme from Jurassic Park."

Dino-Magic Puzzle

Putting dinosaur bones together is a lot like solving a giant jigsaw puzzle! Cut out the pieces and see if you can put this skeleton together the right way. When you've finished, guess which dinosaur these bones belonged to. Then flip over the pieces to see if you were right.

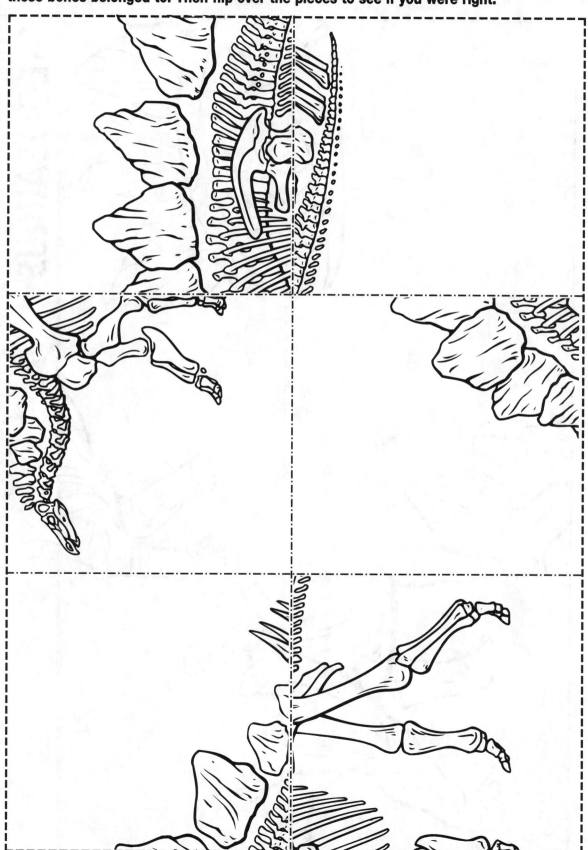

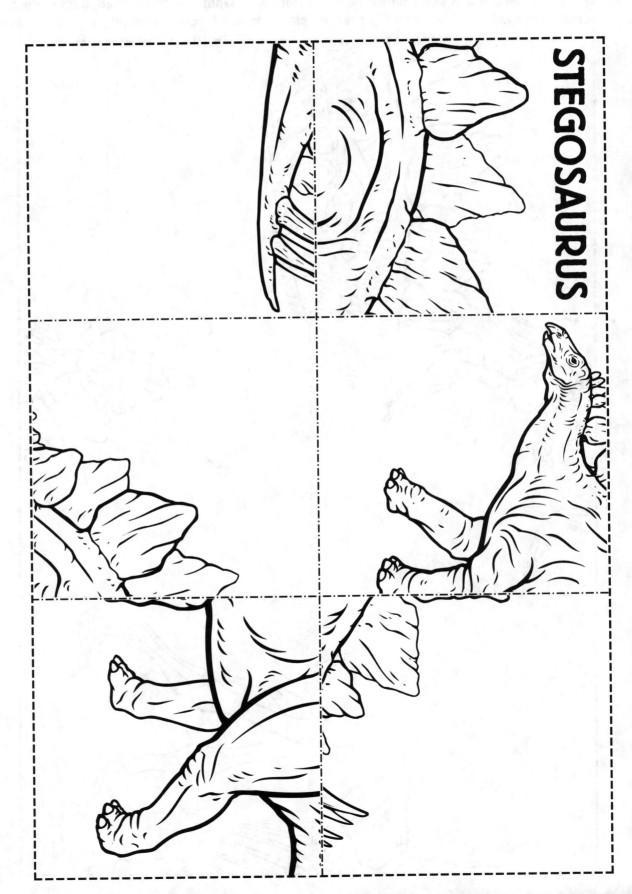

STEGOSAURUS

Name _____

What Tracks Tell Us

Wow, you've discovered some fossilized dinosaur tracks! Study the footprints, then write what you think happened at each site.

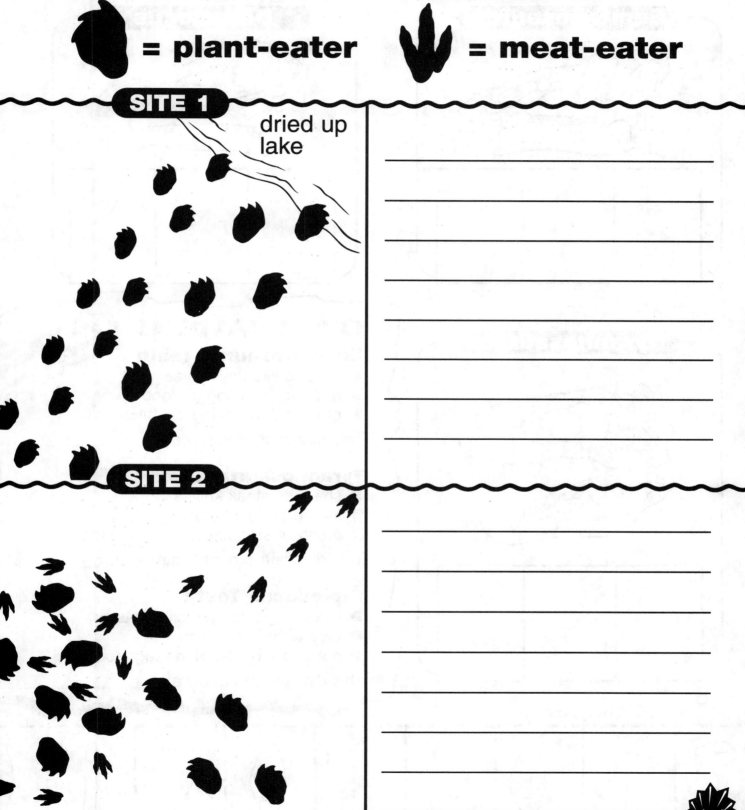

= plant-eater   = meat-eater

SITE 1

dried up lake

SITE 2

What Teeth Tell Us

Pretend you are a paleontologist studying dinosaur teeth. Cut out the teeth at the bottom of the page and paste them next to the dinosaur you think they belong to. Then try to figure out whether each dinosaur ate plants or meat.

Edmontosaurus

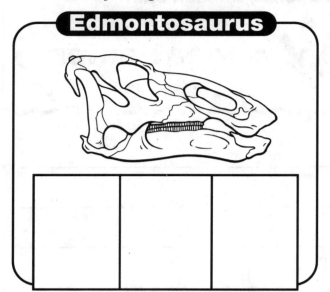

Diplodocus

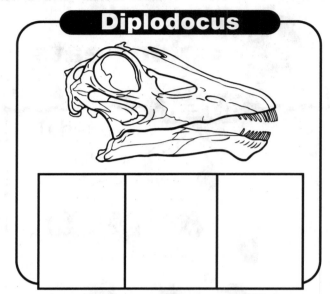

Tyrannosaurus

OBSERVATIONS

Edmontosaurus Teeth
▶ shaped like tiny leaves
▶ good for grinding up food
▶ not good for taking big bites

This dinosaur probably ate_____.

Tyrannosaurus Teeth
▶ sharp as steak knives
▶ strong and powerful
▶ great for stabbing and tearing food

This dinosaur probably ate_____.

Diplodocus Teeth
▶ shaped like dull pencil points
▶ very weak
▶ not good for chewing tough food

This dinosaur probably ate_____.

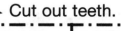 Cut out teeth.

Doing Dinosaur Research

It's your turn to be the paleontologist! A field crew found this skull at a dig site and brought it to the Museum of the Rockies for you to identify. Compare it to some other skulls in the museum's collection to find out what kind of dinosaur it belonged to.

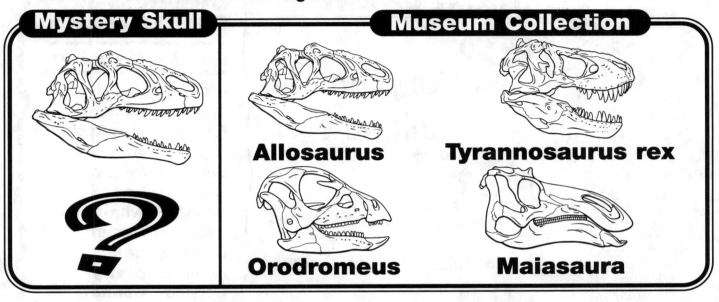

Mystery Skull

Museum Collection

Allosaurus

Tyrannosaurus rex

Orodromeus

Maiasaura

What kind of dinosaur did the skull belong to?_____

Now do some research. Use dinosaur books to answer these questions.

❶ When did your dinosaur live?_____

❷ What does its name mean?_____

❸ What did it eat?_____

❹ What was its length?_____

❺ Where have its bones been found?_____

_____

❻ What other facts did you learn about this dinosaur?

_____

_____

_____

_____

They're All Greek to Me

Most dinosaur names are created by putting two or more Greek words together. Look carefully at the dinosaur pictures below. Then choose a word from the Greek dictionary to describe each one. Connect those words to the Greek word *saurus* (which means "lizard") to name your dinosaurs. We did the first one for you.

NAME CHART

1

Name: <u>Corytho</u>saurus

Meaning: <u>helmet</u> lizard

2

Name:_____saurus

Meaning:_____lizard

3

Name:_____saurus

Meaning:_____lizard

4

Name:_____saurus

Meaning:_____lizard

5

Name:_____saurus

Meaning:_____lizard

GREEK DICTIONARY

Word	Meaning
Allo	**weird**
Anato	**duck**
Ankylo	**crooked**
Archo	**very old**
Baro	**heavy**
Caco	**bad**
Centio	**whale**
Cetio	**monster**
Cephalo	**head**
Compso	**pretty**
Corytho	**helmet**
Donto	**tooth**
Frigo	**cold**
Hadro	**big**
Mega	**great**
Hypsi	**high**
Micro	**small**
Myo	**mouse**
Oro	**mountain**
Ornito	**bird**
Poly	**many**
Psittaco	**parrot**
Pyro	**fire**
Struthio	**ostrich**
Styraco	**spiked**
Rhino	**nose**
Seismo	**earthquake**
Tarbo	**scary**

When you've finished, ask your teacher to tell you what paleontologists have named these dinosaurs. Did you give any of them the same name?

The preparators study the bones to figure out what kind they are and which dinosaur they belonged to. Sometimes they are sent bones that don't fit at all!

A

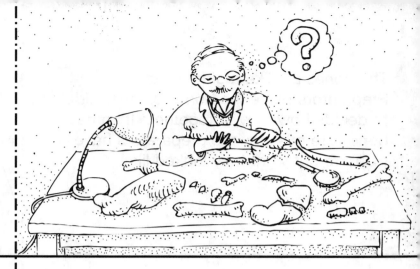

At the museum, other scientists called "preparators" use dental tools and special acids to clean all of the rock from the bones. Sometimes the bones get broken and have to be glued back together again.

B

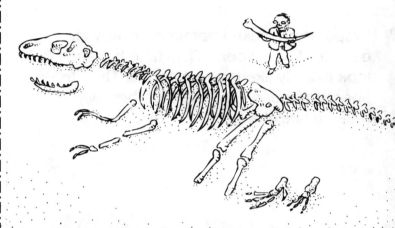

Paleontologists work carefully to remove all of the fossils. In lucky cases, they find lots of bones that belong to the same dinosaur. Those bones are set in casts, packed in crates, and sent to the museum.

C

Paleontologists know the best places to hunt for fossils. When they spot a dinosaur bone peeking out of the ground, they get very excited. They know other bones may be buried there, too.

D

The bones are like a giant puzzle. Preparators place the bones side-by-side to decide how they fit together. If some bones are missing, the preparators have to figure out what they looked like.

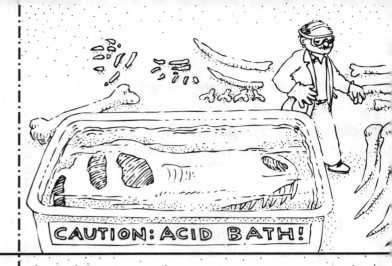

Preparators make fiberglass copies of each and every bone. The fake bones look exactly like the real bones. Then the fiberglass bones are put together to make a skeleton.

The real skeleton is stored in a safe place for scientists to study. The fiberglass skeleton is put on display in a museum. Everybody loves a dinosaur!

MUSEUM DINOSAUR

Ever wonder how dinosaur skeletons end up in museums? Here's my story.

DINO-MITE CERTIFICATE

On this day, _____,
                   Date

_____
Child's Name

is recognized as

an official junior paleontologist.

Congratulations!

MUSEUM OF THE ROCKIES, BOZEMAN, MONTANA

signed:

_____
Teacher

Jack Horner, Curator, Museum of the Rockies

DINOSAUR NAME PRONUNCIATION KEY

Allosaurus: AL-uh-SOR-us
Anatosaurus: ah-NAT-uh-SOR-us
Ankylosaurus: an-KY-luh-SOR-us
Apatosaurus: Ah-PAT-uh-SOR-us
Barapasaurus: ba-RAP-a-SOR-us
Barosaurus: BARE-uh-SOR-us
Brachiosaurus: BRAK-ee-uh-SOR-us
Camarasaurus: KAM-uh-ruh-SOR-us
Ceratosaurus: sair-AT-uh-SOR-us
Centiosaurus: SENT-ee-oh-SOR-us
Chrostenotes: CROW-ste-not-es
Coelophysis: see-luh-FYE-sis
Coelurus: see-LUR-us
Compsognathus: komp-suh-NAY-thus
Corythosaurus: kor-ITH-uh-SOR-us
Daspletosaurus: dass-PLEE-tuh-SAWR-us
Deinonychus: dyne-ON-i-kus
Dimetrodon: dye-MET-ruh-don
Diplodocus: dih-PLOD-uh-kus
Dromiceiomimus: droh-MEE-see-uh-MYE-mus
Dryosaurus: DRY-uh-SOR-us
Edmontosaurus: ed-MONT-uh-SOR-us
Gallimimus: gal-uh-MIME-us
Hadrosaurus: had-ruh-SOR-us
Herrerasaurus: huh-RAYR-uh-SOR-us
Hypacrosaurus: hie-PAK-roe-SOR-us
Hypselosaurus: HIP-se-loh-SOR-us
Iguanodon: ih-GWAN-uh-don
Kentrosaurus: KEN-tro-SOR-us
Lambeosaurus: Lam-bee-uh-SOR-us
Leptoceratops: LEP-toe-SER-a-tops
Lycorhinus: LIE-koe-RINE-us
Maiasaura: Mah-ee-uh-SOR-uh
Megalosaurus: MEG-uh-luh-SOR-us
Monoclonius: MON-uh-KLONE-ee-us

Mussaurus: moo-SOR-us
Nodosaurus: NODE-oh-SOR-us
Opisthocoelicaudia: oh-PIS-thoe-SEEL-ih-KOW-dee-a
Ornitholestes: ore-nith-uh-LESS-teez
Ornithomimus: ore-nith-uh-MEE-mus
Orodromeus: ORE-uh-DROH-mee-us
Oviraptor: oh-vih-RAP-ter
Parasaurolophus: par-a-SOR-uh-LOAF-us
Pachycephalosaurus: pak-ee-SEFF-uh-luh-SOR-us
Plateosaurus: PLAT-ee-uh-SOR-us
Podokesaurus: poh-dok-eh-SOR-us
Polacanthus: pole-uh-KAN-thus
Procompsognathus: pro-komp-suh-NAY-thus
Protoceratops: proh-tuh-SAIR-uh-tops
Psittacosaurus: sit-uh-kuh-SOR-us
Scelidosaurus: skel-LID-uh-SOR-us
Seismosaurus: SYEZ-muh-SOR-us
Spinosaurus: spine-uh-SOR-us
Staurikosaurus: stor-IK-oh-SOR-us
Stegosaurus: steg-uh-SAIR-us
Struthiosaurus: strooth-ee-oh-SOR-us
Styracosaurus: sty-RAK-uh-SOR-us
Technosaurus: TECK-nuh-SOR-us
Therizinosaurus: THER-ih-zin-oh-SOR-us
Titanosaurus: tie-TAN-oh-SOR-rus
Trachodon: TRAK-uh-don
Triceratops: try-SAIR-uh-tops
Troodon: true-OH-don
Tyrannosaurus: ty-RAN-uh-SOR-us
Ultrasaurus: UL-truh-SOR-us
Velociraptor: vel-uh-si-RAP-tor
Vulcanodon: vul-KAN-oh-don
Yaleosaurus: YALE-ee-uh-SOR-us

DINOSAUR RESOURCE LIST

BOOKS FOR EMERGENT READERS

Digging Up Dinosaurs by Aliki (HarperCollins, 1981)
Dinosaur Babies by Maida Silverman (Simon & Schuster, 1988)
Dinosaur Bones by Aliki (HarperCollins, 1984)
Dinosaurs by Gail Gibbons (Holiday House, 1987)
Let's Look at Dinosaurs (Putnam, 1989)
Daniel's Dinosaur by Mary Carmine (Scholastic, 1990)
Dinosaur Day by Liza Donnelly (Scholastic, 1987)

BOOKS FOR FLUENT READERS

Be a Dinosaur Detective by Dougal Dixon (Lerner, 1989)
The Dinosaur Questions and Answer Book by Sylvia Funston (Little, Brown, 1992)
Dinosaurs and How They Lived by Steve Parker (Dorling Kindersley, 1991)
Jack Horner: Living with Dinosaurs by Don Lessem (W.H. Freeman, 1994)
Maia: A Dinosaur Grows Up by Jack Horner and Doug Henderson (Running Press, 1985)
My Life with Dinosaurs by Stephen and Sylvia Czerkas (Pocket Books, 1989)
Why Did the Dinosaurs Disappear? by Dr. Phillip Whitfield (Viking, 1991)

CLASSROOM REFERENCE BOOKS

Dinosaur (An Eyewitness Book) by David Norman, Ph.D. and Angela Milner Ph.D.
   (Knopf, 1989)
The Dinosaur Society Dinosaur Encyclopedia by Don Lessem and Donald F. Glut
   (Random House, 1993)
The Great Dinosaur Atlas by Giuliano Fornari (Dorling Kindersley, 1991)
The New Illustrated Dinosaur Dictionary by Helen Roney Sattler
   (Lothrop, Lee, & Shepard, 1983)

TEACHER RESOURCES

The Big Beast Book by Jerry Booth (Little Brown, 1988)
The Complete T Rex by Jack Horner and Don Lessem (Simon & Schuster, 1993)
D Is for Dinosaur by Patty Abel, Bonnie Sachatello-Sawyer et al.
   (Museum of the Rockies, 1992)
Digging Dinosaurs by Jack Horner and James Gorman (Workman, 1988)
Discover Dinosaurs by Dr. Chris McGowan (Addison Wesley, 1992)
Everything Your Kids Every Wanted to Know About Dinosaurs and You Were Afraid They'd Ask by
   Teri Degler (Carol Publishing, 1990)

PLACES TO SEE DINOSAURS

Academy of Natural Sciences (Philadelphia, PA)
American Museum of Natural History (New York, NY)
Carnegie Museum of Natural History (Pittsburgh, PA)
Denver Museum of Natural History (Denver, CO)
Dinosaur National Monument (Jensen, UT)
Earth Science Museum, Brigham Young University (Provo, UT)
Field Museum of Natural History (Chicago, IL)
Museum of Comparative Zoology, Harvard University (Cambridge, MA)
Museum of Northern Arizona (Flagstaff, AZ)
Museum of the Rockies, Montana State University (Bozeman, MT)
National Museum of Natural History, Smithsonian Institution (Washington, DC)
Natural History Museum (Cleveland, OH)
Stovall Museum, University of Oklahoma (Norman, OK)

ANSWERS

Dinosaurs and You (pages 19 and 20)
Answers will vary, but might include: Alike—Both have eyes, mouth, nose, skin, feet, arms; both walk, eat, have babies, etc. Different—People have hair, soft skin, wear clothes, are alive, can talk, go to school; dinosaurs had scaly skin, tails, were often huge, lived long ago, are now extinct, etc.

1. mandible   **5.** rib
2. skull   **6.** femur
3. digit   **7.** tibia
4: humerus   **8.** metatarsal

What Makes a Dinosaur a Dinosaur? (page 21)
Dinosaurs: *Tyrannosaurus* and *Triceratops*
1. no   **2.** yes   **3.** no

Mesozoic Era Time Line (page 22 and 23)
I'm chasing a lizard: *Coelophysis*
I'm eating a plant: *Plateosaurus*
I've got tall plates on my back: *Stegosaurus*
I'm the smallest dinosaur here: *Compsognathus*
I'm the biggest dinosaur here: *Brachiosaurus*
I've got a spike for a thumb: *Iguanodon*
I've got a big bump on my head: *Corythosaurus*
I've got curled claws on my feet: *Velociraptor*
My nickname is T. rex: *Tyrannosaurus*

The Good Mother (page 44)
1. embryos or baby dinosaurs
2. 10
3. She would crush them.
4. She covered them with plants.
5. Answers will vary, but will include various birds, reptiles, and insects.

Late Cretaceous Food Pyramid (page 47)
Meat-eater: *Tyrannosaurus*
Plant-eaters: *Corythosaurus, Triceratops,* lizard
Plants: horsetail, fern, pine, ginkgo, pine cone, magnolia

Extinction Cartoon Strip (page 48)
See page 40 for correct sequence.

Sorting Out Dinosaurs (Pages 63 and 64)
1. 8, 4; Most of these dinosaurs had bones that were found in the United States.
2. 7, 5; Most of these dinosaurs ate plants.
3. 4, 8; Most of these dinosaurs were more than 20 feet long.
4. 7, 3, 2; Most of these dinosaurs walked on two legs.
5. 2, 3, 7; Most of these dinosaurs lived during the Cretaceous Period. (Note: Fact responses will vary.)

Sizing Up Dinosaurs (page 65)
1. *Brachiosaurus*   **5.** 30 feet
2. *Compsognathus*   **6.** 20 feet
3. 2   **7.** Answers will vary.
4. 10

Dinosaurs Lived Here (page 86)
1. yes   **6.** Antarctica
2. Answers will vary.   **7.** Antarctica
3. 22   **8.** Australia
4. North American   **9.** yes
5. Asia   **10.** no

Picture This!: Dig Site Map (page 89)
teeth: 11; thigh bones: 4; vertebrae: 4; hip bones: 2; skulls: 2
1. teeth   **2.** hip bones, skulls

Dino-Magic Puzzle (page 102) See page 97.

What Tracks Tell Us (page 103)
Answers will vary but might include:
1. Mother and baby plant-eaters went for a drink.
2. Meat-eater attacked a plant-eater.

What Teeth Tell Us (page 104)

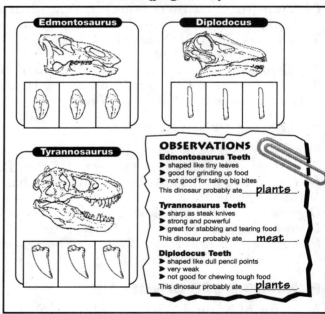

Doing Dinosaur Research (page 105)
The skull belongs to an *Allosaurus.*

They're All Greek to Me (page 106)
1. *Corythosaurus;* helmet lizard
2. *Styracosaurus;* spiked lizard
3. *Centiosaurus;* whale lizard
4. *Psittacosaurus;* parrot lizard
5. *Struthiosaurus;* ostrich lizard